Out Front with Stephen Abram

A GUIDE FOR
INFORMATION
LEADERS

Compiled by
Judith A. Siess and Jonathan Lorig

American Library Association
Chicago   2007

Composition by ALA Editions in Stempel Schneidler and Meta using InDesign CS2.

The paper used in this publication meets the minimum requirements of American National Standard for Information Sciences—Permanence of Paper for Printed Library Materials, ANSI Z39.48-1992. ∞

Library of Congress Cataloging-in-Publication Data
Abram, Stephen.
    Out front with Stephen Abram : a guide for information leaders /
compiled by Judith A. Siess and Jonathan Lorig.
        p.   cm.
    Includes bibliographical references and index.
    ISBN 0-8389-0932-9 (alk. paper)
    1. Libraries and society. 2. Libraries—Information technology.
3. Library users. 4. Library science—Forecasting. I. Siess, Judith A.
II. Lorig, Jonathan. III. Title.
    Z716.4A24 2007
    021.2—dc22   2006031410

ISBN-10: 0-8389-0932-9
ISBN-13: 978-0-8389-0932-4

Printed in the United States of America

11   10   09   08   5   4   3   2

To my wife, Stephanie Smith Abram, with whom everything is possible—SA

To Stephen, without whom this book would not have been possible and who makes the future look very interesting—JAS

Contents

Foreword

Jane Dysart

Can you believe I didn't hire Stephen Abram when I had the chance? It was probably the best thing that could have happened to him, as he has gone on to have a stellar career as a librarian, library manager, electronic publisher, information industry leader, and business executive. He has also become one of my best friends.

We worked together on the 76th annual Special Libraries Association (SLA) conference in Winnipeg. Stephen was the head of the Toronto chapter of the Canadian Association of Special Libraries and Information Services (CASLIS Toronto), and I was the conference chair for SLA. We both had young children at that time and not much life outside of work, the odd library meeting, and our weekly lunches. But we accomplished so much during those lunches. We created workshops and courses to give at the University of Toronto, Ryerson University, SLA, the Medical Library Association (MLA), and the Canadian Library Association (CLA). We discussed what was happening in the information world. We created, with partners, a successful conference—Canada Online—and then sold it. We had fun and we grew. We spread our wings.

Over the years we have continued to "lunch" and work together to push the envelope by creating stimulating talks and workshops, planning conferences, building blogs and wikis, and mentoring and being mentored by others in the information space. When you put curious minds together, they feed off each other, sparking ideas and plans. Stephen has widened his network of curious minds, savvy librarians, and successful information practitioners, especially since joining SirsiDynix as the vice president of innovation. A perfect role and title for Stephen—congratulations to Pat Sommers for recognizing Stephen's strengths!

Stephen has an unbelievable capacity to read and absorb information in so many areas, not just libraries, information, technology, and social behaviors. Don't even ask how many feeds are in his Bloglines. It's scary. We always joke that he has so much minutiae and trivia in his head that we don't know how he retains it. How come he doesn't forget stuff like the rest of us? And not only does he read a lot, but he is also a prolific writer and communicator.

In a world where we are all time-pressured, Stephen has admirably shouldered many volunteer leadership roles, including the presidencies of many associations—the Information Industries Council of the Information Technology Association of Canada, the Ontario Library Association, CASLIS Toronto, CLA, and now SLA. He has spoken to, and influenced, many government officials, industry leaders, publishers, lawyers, and scientists. His opinions and insights are sought after, as witnessed by how much time he spends on the road these days—speaking, listening, and learning. Stephen never stops learning and sharing what he has learned—not just in the information industry, but more personally with many colleagues who are challenged with cancer. He is a cancer survivor and a rock, an anchor, in the information world.

Stephen has a wonderful ability to assimilate huge amounts of information, making connections most people don't even consider, and then leaping to tremendous insights about information organizations, services, and products. He has forecast many an interesting turn in the information industry.

Stephen has a terrific brain, a generous heart, a caring personality, and a huge capacity for learning and doing, as well as a wicked sense of humor. If you've heard him speak at the Computers in Libraries "Dead Technology" session, you know he could have been a comedian, but we're ever so thankful he chose the information industry as his constellation. He is a star. We look forward to more exciting things from Stephen Abram.

Judith A. Siess and Jonathan Lorig

"When Stephen Abram has something to say, particularly about ideas and innovation in our field, you can bet it will be worth paying attention to." So said Luke Rosenberger, technology librarian at the North Harris Montgomery Community College District in Montgomery County, Texas, on October 11, 2005, on http://lbr.library-blogs.net—a blog about virtual reference, created by and for the professional librarians who work for tutor .com's Librarians By Request service.

Stephen Abram has written a lot of material on many subjects. What he writes is always interesting and important for librarians to read, but no one has ever collected his writings in one place. He is on the road at least half of the time, and even though he is usually working on his laptop while he's in the air, he just doesn't have the time to collect them himself. So we decided to do it for him.

Another impetus for this book was reading this quotation of Naomi Baron: "Who's in charge here? It is very common to hear people say here's the Millennial or the digital generation, and we have to figure out how they learn. Poppycock. We get to mold how they learn."* I knew that we had to get the word out to our colleagues that if we try to make the Millennials do things *our* way, it is highly probable that they will just ignore us completely. We have to adapt to the way *they* work and learn, and Abram can be our guide in this effort.

When I first approached him—at the Special Libraries Association's annual conference in Nashville, Tennessee, in June 2004—he was his usual modest self, protesting that "no one would be interested in reading a book about me." Every time I ran into him at the conference, I would ask him again, and every time the people around him said, "That's a great idea!" By the end of the conference I almost had him convinced.

I asked Patrick Hogan, editorial director of ALA Editions, if he would be interested in the book. He was very interested and arranged a meeting with

---

* Naomi Baron, "The Net Generation Goes to College," *Chronicle of Higher Education,* October 7, 2005.

Abram in Chicago to clinch the deal. The American Library Association was chosen to publish the book because they do most of the publishing for the Canadian Library Association, of which Abram is a past president.

If you haven't heard of Stephen Abram, do read his biography later in this book. Here is the short version. Abram has worked in libraries and the information industry for over twenty-five years. He is currently vice president of innovation for SirsiDynix, an industry-leading library automation vendor. He identifies new library, end-user, and information technologies and marketplace trends. He travels worldwide, speaking to SirsiDynix user groups, library association meetings, and other library groups. He also contributes to SirsiDynix's *OneSource* online newsletter, his own blog (*Stephen's Lighthouse*), SLA's *Information Outlook,* and several other librarian-focused publications. He has been recognized as a leader by *Library Journal* magazine and SLA and has served in leadership positions in the Ontario Library Association, CLA, and SLA.

Collecting, selecting, and editing the works of such a prolific author was a daunting task, so I asked Jonathan Lorig to help. We worked together on a previous book (*The Essential OPL, 1998–2004: The Best of Seven Years of "The One-Person Library: A Newsletter for Librarians and Management"*), another compilation. Jonathan has degrees in civil engineering and librarianship; I am a librarian and grew up with and was taught to think by my father, a professor of civil engineering at the University of Illinois at Urbana-Champaign. Both Jon and I are also Illini, so we think alike and work well together. However, since I, like Abram, am a member of the Baby Boom generation and Jonathan is a Gen Xer, we have members of two different generations looking at Abram's work, which made for some interesting discussions about the contents.

Abram and I also think alike; this is probably because we are both anthropologists. Although he studied in Canada and I studied in the United States, we both look at what we're studying using the "participant observer" method we learned as undergraduates. In this method, although we are part of the culture we're studying (librarianship, twentieth- and twenty-first-century library users, students, etc.), we're also observing that culture with as much detachment as possible.

Much of what Abram has written covers more than one subject. In addition, much of what he has developed has been delivered not as written articles or posts on his blog, but as live PowerPoint presentations. We were able to obtain copies of 92 articles and 63 presentations; there are undoubtedly more that we missed. We had to edit and at times do minor rewrites of his notes on these presentations, no easy task. This couldn't do justice to his presentations, so if you get the chance to hear Abram speak—do it! He is even more entertaining, witty, and thought-provoking in person.

We divided this book into four chapters, each related to one of the main themes of Abram's writing. Chapter 1, "Advocacy," contains articles aimed at showing the public (and sometimes librarians) the importance and value of libraries and the professionals who work in them. Chapter 2, "Technology," deals with Abram's fascination with and mastery of technology and how it is—and must be—used to serve library users. Chapter 3, "Communities and Generations," explains Abram's idea of the potential users of the library as divisible into distinct communities. He also writes about the changes in this clientele over time. Abram (and others) discuss the different generations of the twentieth and twenty-first centuries (at least for North America). He focuses on the Millennials, the generation now graduating from college and entering the workforce, both as library users and as librarians. They are markedly different from any generation before, and our profession's response to and acceptance of them will be critical to our survival. This chapter and the next contain the most important of Abram's writings. Chapter 4, "The Future," presents Abram's predictions about and for the future of librarianship, libraries, and librarians. Each chapter's introductory quotation is from Abram's Scholars in Residence presentation at the Chicago Public Library, on November 9, 2005. They are reprinted here as quoted in Michael Stephens's blog, *Tame the Web* (http://tametheweb.com/2005/11/abramisms .html, November 11, 2005).

As you go through this book, you should experience many "aha!" moments—when you read something that you've already seen but hadn't realized its importance before. Stephen Abram has a way of stating the obvious—before we know that it's obvious. That is, what he says is only obvious once he points it out. He seems always to be ahead of our learning curve, seeing things before the rest of us.

—*Judith A. Siess*

Stephen Abram's writings offer fresh thinking and exhibit his willingness to challenge the most popular of ideas. Popularity, he demonstrates, does not necessarily indicate the truth of a statement or the efficacy of a method. For instance, in his *Stephen's Lighthouse* blog entry of August 31, 2005, Abram notes that the cliché phrase "Information wants to be free" actually has been misquoted and misused many times over. I encourage you to see his clear and correct explanation in chapter 1 of this anthology.

We learn also from Abram that societal change is inevitable and that we must seek constantly to understand, to adapt, and to evolve our own behaviors. He wrote in a 2000 *Serials Librarian* article ("Shift Happens") that librarians must reach beyond manuscript collocation and reference services:

"Our goal in the knowledge-based sector is to integrate the data-information-knowledge continuum to fundamentally and positively impact behavior in our enterprises and society. Ecologies require healthy climates and we can be a catalyst in the ultimate health and success of the climate of the knowledge society."

Abram envisions librarians as able agents in the translation of raw information into knowledge for library customers. The writings in this anthology encourage us to productively challenge our methods and thinking. Abram points to the paradigm shifts, specific technologies, and communities through which we can grow together into a culture of experimentation and discovery.

I leave you with an insightful statement by David Carr, associate professor of information and library science at the University of North Carolina at Chapel Hill. During the November 2001 Conference on the 21st Century Learner (sponsored by the Institute of Museum and Library Services), Carr made the following observation: "Our questions are the only ways we have of leading ourselves forward—our only ways to see a common possibility in the promise of cultural institutions. . . . The intelligent evolution of an individual human being requires the cognitive management of informing experiences."

Can our libraries consciously create positive and effective "informing experiences" in the twenty-first century? Stephen Abram would enthusiastically answer yes, and this collection highlights his specific suggestions.

—*Jonathan Lorig*

ACKNOWLEDGMENTS

We thank Patrick Hogan, Jenni Fry, and Christine Schwab at ALA Editions for their efforts, Jane Dysart for writing the foreword, and our families for their unyielding support. We especially thank Stephen Abram for inspiring us with many years of thoughtful writing and for permitting our unrestricted access to those works. We've enjoyed compiling this anthology and have each learned a lot in the process. We hope that the following pages provide learning and value for you too. Enjoy!

One

Advocacy
The Value of Libraries and
How to Explain It to the Public

It's more important to create a community portal than a library website.

Abram has always been a great advocate for libraries and librarians. He has used his "bully pulpit" to promote libraries and to improve the position and image of librarians in the eyes of the public. He worked first at the state level as president of the Ontario Library Association, then at the national level as president of the Canadian Library Association, and now at the international level as the president-elect and then president of the Special Libraries Association. This chapter presents some of his best examples.

This article is a prime example of how Abram is always ahead of his time. It was written in 1993; much of what he envisioned has since come true.

Sydney Claire, SLA Professional Award Winner 2005

Transformational Librarianship in Action

Sydney Claire is an information coach with the Triad Group. In this position, she carries a client load of about ten self-managing work teams at a time. Her role is to use her highly developed information skills to leverage decision making at Triad. The Triad Group, a global corporation operating in all three world triad partners (the Americas bloc, the Pacific Rim, and the EEC), exists as a core decision support organization (DSO; these were called holding companies many years ago) for investments undertaken by itself and its partners to build value for its shareholders.

The date is June 1, 2005—just before the SLA conference in Toronto, Ontario, but available for the first time to all SLA members through the newly arrived Satellite Interactive Connection System, colloquially called the Virtual Conference. Sydney's mind is distracted by notes she is dictating to her personal assistant (PA) in order to create an interactive multimedia presentation for her panel discussion on the use of electronic client profiling as a means of predictive service delivery. She is interrupted by a client call on her video screen, which automatically puts her personal assistant on "call monitor/record" to deal with this higher-priority function.

The client call from Zachary Jared, a team facilitation specialist in Vienna, Austria, is automatically translated into English. Sydney is able to respond to him in English through her Kurzweil translator. He needs to consult with her on how to formulate a query over the Internet to assure maximum response with the fewest false drops. Zachary also wants advice on how to add this

First published in *Special Libraries* 84 (Fall 1993): 213–15.

information effectively to his PA in order to integrate the information automatically with other information collected internally and externally by his work team and with their meeting notes. They were on a deadline and were just about to ask the PA to analyze the data and report on any holes in their work patterns and information search to date.

Sydney was able to counsel Zachary through his Internet queries, and she also used the opportunity to transfer some of her skills to Zachary. She located a little-used utility on the global network that would reprocess his search result and enable him to add it more quickly to his work team's shared files. And finally, Zachary's account was debited automatically for Sydney's services.

As Sydney prepared her presentation, she thought back to her first SLA conference and how things had changed in twenty years. She considered how large a role SLA had played in providing the leadership her chosen profession needed to develop the skills, behaviors, and attitudes that were now required for success in the many jobs information professionals now held. Indeed, she first fully understood the term *information professional* at an early SLA conference. In fact, the SLA president's Task Force on the Value of the Information Professional is now regarded as a turning point in helping special librarians understand the true worth of information service.

Sydney well remembers the turbulence in the profession in the 1990s as information became the only remaining success lever for business. Some of her colleagues were unable to make the transition from effective library manager to transformational librarian, and the SLA's leadership struggled through the 1990s to understand and redefine the image of the information professional and to further research the value equation for information. All of this accelerated at the 1994 conference with the announcement of a new vision for the future of SLA and the profession. The vision—rooted in the values first espoused by John Cotton Dana and shared throughout the history of the profession—provided the touchstone needed to focus on the key competencies required for success in the future. Sydney remembers being excited by the vision at first, then skeptical that the profession could really embrace the vision without the information parade passing it by, and then being thrilled at how her association implemented it.

Sydney recalls the international education program for all SLA members delivered throughout the 1990s in preparation for the millennium. SLA members were proud to see the leadership of their association held up as a model of active paradigm shifters, ahead of many industries who struggled to embrace the ever more rapidly changing environment. The nub of the program was to add certain core competencies to the profession that it would sorely need for success in the Information Age—competencies that were not entirely understood or appreciated when the majority of Sydney's colleagues received their professional education.* These training opportunities were based on the premise that the future would require four key competencies.

True information literacy. Not merely technological or computer literacy, not the entry-level skills of numeracy or language literacy, or just research and communication skills—but the ability to combine a deep understanding of information dynamics with advanced interpersonal and empathy skills to deliver answers that support client decisions.

Selling skills. Not just marketing ability. Since information was now the commodity that drove the economies of the triad, it was now essential that leaders in the information industry be completely at ease with pricing and closing the sales of information transactions.

Affiliative abilities. How things had changed through the 1990s with respect to what used to be clear competition among corporations. Alliances among companies were now the norm, especially after it became clear that acquisitions did little to build wealth and much to churn money without adding value. The ability to construct on-the-fly temporary, and sometimes long-term, alliances between information industry players (including vendors, intellectual property creators, copyright owners, libraries, etc.) was essential to create the multimedia, multidimensional packages clients now demanded.

Strategic thinking. Sydney's corporation was not unique in that it had adopted the biological model of organization, meaning that its structure more closely resembled a model of an organic molecule, with pieces allying and breaking off as needs demanded. Indeed, with few exceptions, nearly all "units" were shared with other organizations, and the lines had blurred over the years so that one organization ended where another began. This meant that certain core competencies were valued more highly than others. The organization now placed a much lower value on traditional managerial and supervisory skills and a higher value on analytical and critical thinking skills, advanced networking and teamwork abilities, independent work styles, information-handling skills, and communication skills that went beyond the "excellent oral and written communication skills" cliché of Sydney's early career.

All of these training opportunities were colored by the belief that the 1990s and beyond would feature accelerated change on all fronts, and that truly successful information professionals could take the dimension of time into account in their research and produce information packages that were so proactive that their content would be largely predictive. The information professionals who most fully developed this skill were in the highest demand. Many organizations lived by the precept that "if you cannot think

---

* The SLA competencies for twenty-first-century information professionals, formulated by a group led by Joanne Marshall, weren't published until 1996. —Eds

about the future, you cannot have one," and understood that they had to live in the future for almost all decisions—and that the only proven reducer of risk for this strategy was effective use of information.

Sydney thought back to when she got her MLS in 1989. In those halcyon days she had looked forward to working her way up to running a large banking library, or perhaps in another business information center. Now she thought of her colleagues and how few of them actually worked in what could be called "traditional" special library environments. Indeed, few organizations even had those kinds of libraries anymore, although they almost always had more "librarians" than they did in the past. She remembered all those unproductive debates about calling her profession "librarianship," and how many of her colleagues declared that they were no longer "librarians" as soon as they were promoted out of the "library." Her colleagues noticed that CPAs didn't declare themselves "no longer CPAs" when they became bank presidents, and professional engineers were still engineers when they led the big oil companies. In the dawn of the Information Age, Sydney began to think that being a professional librarian wasn't such a bad thing.

Sydney had learned in an SLA course how to really communicate effectively with the numbers people. At library school she learned the importance of statistics. Unfortunately, the drill hadn't included what to do with all of these wonderful stats! SLA focused on the importance of measurement—measuring the right things, using these measurements to communicate to management, measuring value, measuring success, and measuring the relationship of the library's functions to the organization's mission and goals. Learning the real purpose of statistics—to measure success, and not to use them as a defensive tactic to ward off downsizing initiatives from management—had freed Sydney to reevaluate what her library should do, and not just defend what it did. Sydney was ready to tackle the future.

This reflection upon her roots gave Sydney the energy she needed to get back to her presentation. She worried, as she had for twenty years, that there were always librarians who knew more than she did about her topic. Was she really a so-called "expert"? She worried how she would look on the monitor across the world and how she would sound in simultaneous translation—they hadn't quite perfected the emotionless voices of the translators, which made using humor chancy. Then she felt a quick rush of anxiety when she realized that in ten years the SLA conference speakers might be projected as three-dimensional holograms, too!

Her reverie ended as her PA called with another assignment. She glanced at the plaque over her kitchen table and read Triad's motto. . . .

> Information not books
>
> Answers not information
>
> Decisions not answers.

The Really Big Picture

If you want to damage a culture—attack its libraries. Libraries can be as strong as a tree, but they're as fragile as a flower. The great Indian librarian, Ranganathan, asserted, in one of his five laws, that libraries are a growing organism. Once they cease to grow and develop and evolve, they cease to be great libraries. In today's society, we must attack the assumption that everything can be expressed effectively on a spreadsheet as having a clear economic value. Not everything needs to be seen strictly through the business case lens. Jane Jacobs argued effectively for balance in her book *Systems of Survival,* where public and private space overlap and all players need to be kept in balance for a successful society. Libraries are major contributors to this balance. The pirates of the new millennium are trying to monetize everything and everyone as a paying customer. Libraries must speak eloquently for the rights of citizens to unfettered access to information, privacy protection, Canadian culture, and more in a free democracy. We stand on the side of angels when we speak for intellectual freedom, protection of culture, learning, research, workplace information, the success of our neighborhoods, and more. This is not just our passion; it is our responsibility as a profession. And that is the *big picture.* So when anyone—some special interest, budget demon, or politician—launches an attack on libraries, let's make no mistake, this is an attack on freedom, democracy, and our culture. When the unenlightened attack or close or

First published in *OLA* (Ontario Library Association) *Access,* March 2005.

understaff or underfund school libraries, they are attacking the future of our culture and the learning capacity of our schools and kids. When a public library's branches are threatened for purely budgetary reasons, it's an attack on our communities and neighborhoods. When budget demons suggest that a community can only have what it can afford—despite other communities offering better services to their citizens and taxpayers—it's an attack on those residents' ability to succeed and participate equitably in our nation. When colleges and universities don't have the resources that they need to build the next generation, do applied and theoretical research, and provide an environment for free thinking, then our culture is under attack at a most fundamental level.

When you want to attack a culture—whether you're American or British invaders, Taliban insurgents, revolutionaries, or conquistadores—you attack that culture's storehouses of culture, its libraries. And Mother Nature can destroy, and all the food and medicine and rebuilt homes cannot restore that culture until the libraries return. And when libraries are hurt by a thousand cuts thoughtlessly promulgated by shallow-thinking or unthinking bureaucrats or politicians, we must not let it pass without calling them to task and shining a great light on their stupidity.

Our cultures are not trivial—art, film, reading, poetry, fiction, plays, music, entertainment, and more—they all represent the expressions of our diversity of thought and philosophy that make the entire world so magical. Libraries animate that culture for all time. In this period of energizing change, we must remember this basic big picture and protect against any challenges to the basic premise of why libraries exist. I took a few courses once about being a change agent. One lesson has always remained with me—"Culture trumps everything." If you endanger the repositories of our culture, you endanger everything.

The library movement is part of protecting human culture. Be a part of it.

As president of the Canadian Library Association, Abram
wrote a monthly column in their magazine, *Feliciter*,
which usually dealt with some form of advocacy.

Rediscover the Library Movement

Inaugural Address of Stephen Abram,
CLA President 2004–2005, Victoria,
British Columbia, June 2004

I took a decidedly different approach to my inaugural address. I didn't speak
from a prepared text. Those who know my speaking style may have been
surprised that there were no PowerPoint slides. There was no podium.
There were, however, candles. I just chatted with the celebration gala
guests and wandered about the beautiful ballroom of the Empress Hotel.
I tried to share my passion for libraries, the work of library workers, and
the role we play in society. Whether I was successful or not is a matter for
debate. What isn't debatable is that I am passionate about our profession,
our institutions, and Canada. Hence, my focus will be to spend this year
reconnecting with one another, with our partner associations in the prov-
inces and territories, and with a revitalized Canadian library movement.

CANDLES AS A SYMBOL

I chose to use candles at each table in Victoria and leave them unlit throughout dinner. After dinner I went about the ballroom lighting each table's
candles. Why? Candles are an almost universal symbol, and several candle
metaphors are apt to our situation.

First, candles seem to be involved in nearly every human celebration.
We must celebrate our role and achievements more in Canadian libraries.

We mustn't keep our candles under a basket! We must speak up in all
the dark corners of our country. Libraries make a difference.

First published in *Feliciter,* September–October 2004.

Second, Jack was nimble, Jack was quick, and Jack jumped over a candlestick. On the whole, the Canadian library movement needs to work on being more nimble and quick while retaining our strengths in thoughtfulness and research. We need to learn not to study something to death—we must execute our plans! Hence, we must focus this year on achieving progress in our strategic plan. This means taking action in the absence of perfect information. It is time for libraries and library workers to look after ourselves and take risks in the name of our cause. We made some progress this year in the area of advocacy on the political front. Just before our annual conference in Victoria, we sent a letter to every candidate in the federal election. We built a government relations plan. We are nonpartisan, but we are biased and that's OK. We must also light a few candles on the professional learning and community networking fronts this year.

Third, candles are fire—and we might want to consider lighting a fire under our butts. If we don't stand up for our values and speak up, no one else will. We believe in intellectual freedom, the power of school libraries, the role of unfettered access to information in a democracy, balance in copyright laws, and more. Threats to libraries and information rights are direct threats to Canadian values, democracy, and our way of life. CLA needs to be there on these issues and, yes, this includes everything from library budget and financing issues to the threat of entire generations growing up thinking that "to Google is to research well." Not!

THE POWER OF ONE

That evening in Victoria I celebrated the achievements of my colleagues—as individuals, as collaborators, and as leaders. I could not talk about everyone I admire, and in this column I can't even cover everyone I mentioned that night. I would, however, like to note the accomplishments of a few individuals who have made a difference.

For example, I celebrated Ken Haycock, librarian extraordinaire, but specifically his work in assembling the powerful research that shows the key positive role school libraries play in student performance.

I celebrated Canadian library advocate Pat Cavill, who was recently named the first recipient of the new ALA Award for Advocacy.

And what can one say about Ernie Ingles—a great Canadian bibliographer, a true leader in the founding of the Northern Exposure to Leadership Institute, and a man with his hand ever present in initiatives and studies like the 8 Rs, digital libraries, historical microfilm, and more. Ernie is always assembling groups of friends and colleagues around great ideas and initiatives, and he achieves so much for libraries in Canada.

Wendy Newman, one of CLA's great past presidents, has influenced the development of broadband connectivity nationwide, turned the Brantford Public Library into a world-renowned UNESCO site, and is now at the University of Toronto attending to creating the next generation of librarians. Cool!

Our ability to collaborate on ever-increasing levels of complexity is exemplified by the work of folks like Deb deBruijn and others who have created big honking visions of library infrastructures—like the Alberta Library, the Ontario Digital Library, Novanet, and CNSLP—to support the needs of all Canadians. These are amazing visions, and we're getting closer to even greater achievements every year. It's the power of one.

At CLA in Victoria we had the opportunity to see, hear, and meet Skawennio Barnes and Kim Delormier. Skawennio lobbied from the age of thirteen for a library on her reserve, Kahnawake. She won, against great odds. Her story is inspirational and reminds us that libraries are not just for librarians. They can be created by the smallest and most challenged of communities to meet their learning, research, and recreational needs. All it took was her shared vision, effort, and persistence. It's the power of one.

Lastly, CLA would be remiss if we did not honor the life of Jack McClelland, who passed away just before our conference. Without his vision of a truly Canadian publishing house and the creation of the New Canadian Library series, a vehicle for Canadian authors to remain in print, we wouldn't have been able to teach, collect, and enjoy CanLit as a discipline. One man, allied with like-thinking colleagues and friends, made a difference. Canadian culture is enhanced for his having lived.

All of these folks represent the ability of a single individual to serve as a catalyst for a group of friends and colleagues—their network—to achieve higher goals. It's the power of one.

It's also why CLA exists—for individual members to achieve great things with friends and colleagues. CLA's emphasis will be on execution this year, on what you told us you wanted and endorsed in all those surveys: advocacy, networking, and continuing learning opportunities. Library workers are a keystone species in the information ecology and the knowledge-based economy. Not a huge group, but essential and critical for economic and social success. However, if we don't upgrade and update our skills—through all kinds of learning, conference, and networking opportunities—we can't sustain our success. We must prepare future library leaders and library workers. Like last year, we will try to visit every library program we can in Canada. Students are our future and we need to invest in them.

I often say, "Would those of you who say it can't be done please get out of the way of those of us who are already doing it?" The corollary of this is that no one part of the library world can point to another part and tell them that their side of the boat is sinking. We're all in this boat together, and divided we will sink. Please volunteer, share your ideas, contribute to discussion lists, and write. CLA cannot do it without you.

I look forward to working with members, staff, and council in the coming year. We have a great team, and it will be an exciting roller-coaster ride as we build toward another great conference in Calgary in 2005, the 100th anniversary of Alberta's entrance into the Confederation. Please plan today to be at CLA's Calgary conference, where our theme will be about rediscovering and reconnecting with your passion for libraries and the work of libraries. Light a candle. Rediscover the library movement!

The Value of Libraries

Impact, Normative Data,
and Influencing Funders

INTRODUCTION

I've been thinking a lot about the role that libraries play in society and the
impact we have—for good or evil—in how society works and progresses.
I was moved by the impact of a story that I heard at ALA Midwinter 2005,
which I will paraphrase here.

Sharon Terry has an amazing story. Terry tells a story that makes it crystal clear why libraries must be at the front of open access and unfettered
access for research and learning. Terry and her husband became activists
through a very personal route. She was a college pastor and her husband a
construction worker. Their two young children were both diagnosed with
a rare form of cancer and were given little hope of any course other than
the loss of their eyesight and other complications. At the ALA conference
she described the hoops she had to go through to access publicly supported
libraries and databases in search of a cure for her children. She schemed
to become an "authorized user," paid fees, fines, ILL fees, etc. At some
points she had to resort to borrowing and stealing passwords to access
content. In the end, despite library policies but because libraries exist, she
succeeded—and how! Terry and her husband researched the medical literature, built a definitive chart of the disease, patented the gene they found
was responsible for the disease, and wrote articles that were published in
the prestigious medical journal *Nature*. Despite being laypeople, they did

First published in *SirsiDynix OneSource,* April 23, 2006 (http://www.imakenews.com/
sirsi/e_article000396335.cfm).

quite well with the research literature once they got their hands on it. They formed the Genetic Alliance (http://www.geneticalliance.org), an international coalition of advocacy groups that has collected hundreds of case studies on parents and advocates who have suffered from the lack of open access to current medical literature. Terry also formed the Alliance for Taxpayer Access (http://www.taxpayeraccess.org) to secure public access to research funded by taxpayer dollars, especially through the U.S. National Institutes of Health (NIH). More examples presented by Terry demonstrate the importance of open access and the particularly obvious case for open access to publicly funded research results. She responds bluntly to the charge that the NIH proposal will harm the financial stability of publishers, saying, "Since when is the NIH/government in the business of ensuring the sustainability of companies?"

There's a happy ending to this story. Today, the Terrys' children are doing well, and the treatments that their parents vigorously pursued have worked. Some at ALA Midwinter were moved to tears—some by the simple story of the power of research, others, I suspect, in fear of how many have been hurt by library rules that restrict access to our collections and services.

So, as I said, this story got me thinking about proofs of how the unfettered access to information and information services makes a difference in our various communities: public libraries, school libraries, university and college libraries, and special libraries. What is the real value of public, academic, school, and special libraries? Here are the highlights of what I found. I've included a selected webliography at the end of the article so you can enjoy the reading more too.

VALUE OF PUBLIC LIBRARIES

"Dividends: The Value of Public Libraries in Canada," a study done in 1996–97, was a seminal work in exploring the impact—both soft and hard measures—of public libraries on communities in Canada. Key conclusions were that

> Public libraries have an increasing role to play in Canada.
>
> Public libraries, however, are under increasing financial pressures.
>
> Public libraries are cost-effective information providers.
>
> The value and importance of information is increasing.
>
> Public libraries support the local economy.
>
> Public libraries support the cultural industry sector.
>
> Public libraries support Canadian culture.

Public libraries support a democratic society.

Public libraries support and promote literacy.

Public libraries support children and students.

Public libraries support lifelong learning.

Public libraries help bridge the digital divide.

Pretty powerful stuff! Many of the measures in this study were soft or polling data, with some anecdotal stories to support the conclusions. I understand that a new study is under serious consideration by the Canadian Urban Libraries Council. This would clearly be a most welcome update.

Recently, several jurisdictions have taken library system impact measures to another level. In September 2004, a comprehensive taxpayer ROI (return-on-investment) study on the impact of public libraries in Florida found

Overall, Florida's public libraries return $6.54 for every $1.00 invested from all sources (all figures are US$).

For every $6,448 spent on public libraries from public funding sources in Florida, one job is created.

For every dollar of public support spent on public libraries in Florida, gross regional product increases by $9.08.

For every dollar of public support spent on public libraries in Florida, income (wages) increases by $12.66.

Another major study—released in January 2005 in South Carolina by the School of Library and Information Science at the University of South Carolina in collaboration with the South Carolina Association of Public Library Administrators and cooperatively with the South Carolina State Library on the impact of public libraries—found indications that the public library

Improved overall quality of life: 92 percent said yes.

Increased local property values: 47 percent said yes.

Attracted new businesses to the community: 38 percent said yes.

Attracted patronage to local businesses: 44 percent said yes.

Enhanced personal fulfillment: 73 percent said yes.

Nurtured a love of reading: 73 percent said yes.

Was a source of personal enjoyment: 64 percent said yes.

Helped manage personal finances or saved money: 32 percent said yes.

Helped to obtain a new job: 11 percent said yes.

Helped improve or start business: 15 percent said yes.

Helped with a business opportunity: 25 percent said yes.

Assisted workers to be more productive in their jobs: 37 percent said yes.

Introduced users to new technologies: 28 percent said yes.

Helped users with primary education work: 18 percent said yes.

Helped users with lifelong learning: 47 percent said yes.

Contributed to their homeschooling efforts: 12 percent said yes.

Forty-nine percent of business users indicated that they obtained most of their business/research information from the public library.

Seventy-eight percent of business users indicated that information obtained from the public library contributed to the success of their business.

Without access to the information in their public library, 23 percent of business users indicated that they estimated their costs would increase between $500 and $5,000, and 7 percent estimated their costs would increase by $5,000.

Forty-one percent of business users said that if they did not have access to the public library it would have some negative impact, and 33 percent said it would have a major negative impact on their business.

Fifty-nine percent of personal investors said they obtained the information needed for making investment decisions from their public library.

Forty-eight percent said "definitely" the investment information at the public library had contributed to their financial well-being, and 34 percent said "somewhat."

Thirty-two percent of the respondents said the dollar value of the information obtained from the public library was between $10,000 and $1,000,000, and 2 percent said it was over $1,000,000.

Among the economic impact findings are the following [http://www.libsci.sc.edu/SCEIS/exsummary.pdf]:

1. The direct economic impact of all South Carolina public library expenditures is $80,000,000.

2. The existence of South Carolina public libraries brings to the state (from federal and private sources) almost $5 million each year that it would not otherwise have.

3. The value of the loans and use of books, videos, cassettes, CDs, newspapers, magazines, etc., to users each year is approximately $102 million.

4. The value of reference services to users in South Carolina each year is approximately $26 million.

5. The total *direct* economic impact of South Carolina public libraries is estimated at $222 million, while the actual cost of these services to the state and local governments is only $77.5 million. This means that for every $1.00 spent by state and local governments on South Carolina public libraries, the return on investment is $2.86.

6. The *indirect* economic impact of South Carolina public library expenditures (wages, supplies, books and related materials, construction, etc.) on the state's economy is almost $126 million. This means that for every $1.00 expended by South Carolina public libraries, the state receives $1.62 of indirect economic impact.

7. The total direct and indirect return on investment for every $1.00 expended on the state's public libraries by South Carolina state and local governments is $4.48—almost 350 percent!

Glen Holt, of the St. Louis Public Library, has written numerous studies on libraries' role in the community. There are other studies across the land.

There may never be enough of these impact studies. There are certainly too many if we don't use the data to influence the folks who control the purse strings! Read them and use what you need. If they're not right on for what you need, then do your own study, talk to your library schools and encourage more research, contract the survey you need. . . .

VALUE OF ACADEMIC AND COLLEGE LIBRARIES

The value of academic libraries is often strongly tied to the value of colleges and universities themselves. There are many reports on the impact of universities and colleges and higher education on the economics of a community.

In this particular sector, I am fond of a study called "Libraries Designed for Learning" by Scott Bennett. This is an articulate report on what needs to be considered to place the library at the heart of the new university—virtual and bricks. As we create information and learning commons we need to consider many new and mutated issues (including our Millennial users), and this report is a good place to start.

Another study that makes a good point is OCLC's "White Paper on the Information Habits of College Students." This excellent, free study provides data on students' preferences in dealing with the library and research information. It concludes with some tough questions for libraries and library staff to ponder strategically.

What should libraries' strategies be if students

> Prefer web access from home?
>
> Naturally gravitate toward the most popular web tools?
>
> Prefer single-point access using web search engines?
>
> Want assistance any way at all—although they prefer personal and face-to-face?
>
> Want access to resources—wherever they are or whoever owns them?
>
> Clearly want to know more about library services?
>
> Base their opinion and perceptions of library service on evening and weekend experiences?

"The Digital Disconnect: The Widening Gap between Internet-Savvy Students and Their Schools" (August 14, 2002) and "The Internet Goes to College: How Students Are Living in the Future with Today's Technology" (September 15, 2002), both from the Pew Internet and American Life Project, are based on decent data. It's scary data, too. There is emerging proof of a severe generation gap between students and the teachers, professors, and librarians who serve them in their learning environment. Some might say that's just the students' perception and they need to learn more. But great marketers live by the adage that "perception is reality," since few individuals differentiate between their real and false perceptions.

"Dimensions and Use of the Scholarly Information Environment" from CLIR/DLF was published after the Digital Library Federation and the Council on Library and Information Resources commissioned Outsell, Inc., to conduct a large-scale study of undergraduates, graduate students, and faculty members from academic institutions in order to better understand how users' expectations of libraries are changing. A summary report, including 158 tables, is available online. This report is fascinating in its detail about how students, professors, and librarians are using electronic resources, from e-journals and the OPAC to the Web and subscription databases.

I do worry that my research finds too few empirical studies of the broader role of the college and university library on learning and research in the academic setting. Are they just difficult to find? Is the position of the academic library so unassailable that the research isn't needed? I wonder.

VALUE OF SPECIAL LIBRARIES

Having spent many years in a special library setting, I am all too aware of the position in which special libraries are placed—you're only as good as your last reference question or research project. You are under constant pressure to justify your services, role, and budget in the specialized environment in which you practice.

There are quite a few studies on the value of special librarians and their services. However, each is often narrowly focused, and its results are limited to the sector in which it was done.

Two examples which I particularly admire were accomplished by Joanne Gard Marshall. The first sought to discover the impact of the medical library on the decisions of doctors. It's referred to as the "Rochester Study." In 1991, physicians were asked to request some information related to a current, real clinical case and then to evaluate its impact on the care of their patients. There were fifteen participating hospitals. As a result of the information provided by the library, 80 percent of the 208 physicians who returned their questionnaires said that they probably or definitely handled some aspect of patient care differently than they would have handled it otherwise. Specific changes that were reported by the physicians were

Diagnosis	29 percent
Choice of Tests	51 percent
Choice of Drugs	45 percent
Reduced Length of Hospital Stay	19 percent
Advice Given to the Patient	72 percent

Physicians also said that the services and information provided by the library contributed to their ability to avoid the following:

Hospital Admission	12 percent
Patient Mortality	19 percent
Hospital-Acquired Infection	8 percent
Surgery	21 percent
Additional Tests or Procedures	49 percent

Yes! You do see in these data that working with medical libraries avoided patient mortality. Librarians save lives too! Excitingly, the physicians rated the information provided by the library more highly than that provided by other information sources such as diagnostic imaging, lab tests, and discussions with colleagues.

Professor Marshall also performed another impact study for SLA in 1995. She studied the impact of the library on corporate decision making in the five major Canadian banks. This study, published by SLA, shows powerful impacts of library-delivered research and reference on decisions having total impacts of over one million dollars each. The impacts usually changed the course of the research of the end user and/or saved significant money.

There are other studies that have been done in the fields of patents and in pharmaceuticals that show the impact of the library on improving regulatory compliance and speeding approvals from authorities, for example.

Again, there is too little hard-core research and study, but what is out there is very compelling.

VALUE OF SCHOOL LIBRARIES

In the school library field, there are numerous studies and seemingly increasing stupidity in just ignoring them. I heard the word *anegnosis* once. It's similar to *amnesia,* although instead of forgetting knowledge and experience, it means to willfully ignore or be unaware of facts and knowledge. Ken Haycock's summary of the major studies, internationally, was published in 2003 by the Canadian Coalition for School Libraries. It clearly shows that students who attend schools with well-funded, properly stocked libraries managed by qualified teacher-librarians have higher achievement, improved literacy, and greater success at the postsecondary level. Duh! So why are we having a crisis in school libraries, where they're threatened routinely?

The study is entitled "The Crisis in Canada's School Libraries: The Case for Reform and Reinvestment." "The evidence is there for all to see," says Haycock, professor and former director at the graduate School of Library, Archival and Information Studies at the University of British Columbia. "That's why governments in the U.S., Europe, and Asia are aggressively investing in their school libraries. What's disturbing is that Canadian policy makers are ignoring the findings of literally decades of research that shows why school libraries and qualified teacher-librarians are essential components in the academic programming of any school." Standardized scores tend to be 10 to 20 percent higher than in schools without an investment in a school library program. "The relationship between library resource levels and increased achievement is not explained away by other school variables (e.g., per student spending, teacher-pupil ratios) or community conditions (e.g., poverty, demographics). In fact, no fewer than forty years of research—conducted in different locations, at different levels of schooling, in different socioeconomic areas, sponsored by different agencies, and conducted by different, credible researchers—provides an abundance of evidence about the *positive* impact of qualified teacher-librarians and school libraries on children and adolescents."

Two leading U.S. researchers in the field offer this arresting conclusion: "In research done in nine states and over 3,300 schools since 1999, the positive impact of the school library program is consistent. [They] make a difference in academic achievement. If you were setting out a balanced meal for a learner, the school library media program would be part of the main course, not the butter on the bread" (Lance and Loertscher 2003).

We need to continue to get the word out. The Ontario Library Association has committed Can$100,000 to the completion of an Ontario study on the impact of the school library on learners. This will add more Canadian content to the corpus of evidence-based research proving the relationship of teacher-librarians, school library workers, and school libraries to the success of students.

Again, it will all be for naught if we don't promote it and build understanding in the education decision-making communities. We need to be at the table, and we need to be heard. Support the advocacy efforts of our fellow professionals in the library movement.

OCLC ADVOCACY INITIATIVE

In recent years, OCLC has gifted the library community with many items of value. They have launched an advocacy campaign to raise awareness of critical library issues and to help libraries demonstrate their value. The OCLC Environmental Scan and the "Libraries: How They Stack Up" document are examples of tools that can be used by libraries to influence their communities and funding bodies.

NORMATIVE DATA PROJECT FROM SIRSI AND FLORIDA STATE UNIVERSITY

Today, most of the information available on libraries is just that: information *on libraries*. It is not information about *what goes on inside libraries*. It's what's inside libraries, either inside our buildings or inside our web presence, that *is exciting* and tells a wonderful story.

In January 2005 Sirsi Corporation launched the Normative Data Project for Libraries (http://www.librarynormativedata.info). Designed to help libraries analyze collections and collection use across a large, normalized set of library data, the Normative Data Project (NDP) represents a unique opportunity to standardize and amass a centralized data warehouse containing actual circulation and collections data from contributing North American public libraries.

This NDP is jointly created by leading library community organizations, including hundreds of libraries in North America, the GeoLib Program at Florida State University, and Sirsi Corporation. The goals of this cooperative effort are to compile transaction-level data from libraries throughout North America; to link library data with geographic and demographic data on communities served by libraries; and thereby to empower library decision makers to compare and contrast their institutions with real-world industry norms on circulation, collections, finances, and other parameters. Census, integrated library system, and National Center for Education Statistics data are added into the system for comparison purposes.

"Libraries today must find ways to optimize operations, maximize resources, enhance services, extend 'market' penetration, and serve 'customers,'" said Patrick Sommers, Sirsi's chief executive officer. "Having access to real-world data on trends and dynamics impacting a broad spectrum of libraries means that library community leaders can conduct benchmarking, manage collections, prepare budgets, choose facility sites, and make other decisions with greater insight than ever before possible."

Already, more than 700 library outlets—representing approximately 300 North American library systems with a combined annual income of more than $340 million and combined annual circulation in excess of 150 million items—are contributing data to the project. Data for 10.5 million unique titles and 30 million copies are contained in these libraries' collections, which are valued collectively at more than $1 billion. Additional libraries continue to be added, with plans to have data from approximately 500 library systems and 2,500 library outlets in the NDP database this year. The most important difference between the NDP initiative and other sources of information on libraries is that it is not survey-based data. NDP is based on detailed transaction-level, operational data maintained day-to-day in libraries' integrated library systems. In other words, NDP doesn't just provide information *on* libraries. It reveals what actually goes on inside libraries. For example, there are many sources that provide total circulation figures for libraries, but they provide no insight into what materials are being circulated. NDP will provide a broader understanding of libraries and their operations than previously possible by providing—even down to the call-number level—what materials are being circulated where and to whom. No individual-specific data is gathered or maintained by NDP, so as to protect the personal privacy of individual library users.

"For more than a decade, the GeoLib Program has been focused on bringing to bear the power of geographic and demographic information for library decision makers," said Christie Koontz, the director of GeoLib. "Why is geographic and demographic information so important for libraries? Because, just like other businesses, libraries need to know who and where their customers are," said Koontz. "Now, with the Normative Data Project, another dimension is added—library decision makers can view and analyze the actual behavior of library users."

Library leaders and other organizations, companies, or individuals interested in accessing data and reports from NDP have been able to do so online since 2005. Top-level statistics for the library community are available free of charge, along with a range of valuable resources. Access to NDP's full reporting and analyses capabilities is provided on subscription.

This vendor/library/academic partnership represents a unique opportunity to create ongoing measurements and norms for library operations to effectively track change, manage operations, and build funding justifications. It's very exciting.

CONCLUSION

These are challenging times for libraries. We need to communicate our value strongly and in many ways. The studies and opportunities outlined above are fabulous initiatives. We must take our basic statistics and turn them into measurements, and then we must share our measurements. Raw statistics are just representations of effort—something bureaucrats view with cost-cutting eyes. Well-chosen measurements can demonstrate the amazing value and impact of libraries to their communities, host organizations, and funders. All players—vendors, publishers, library workers, institutions, and communities—in the information space have a vested interest to ensure that we communicate this impact and value well. Finally, we must enliven these measurements with the real-life experiences of our users. We must share our stories and provide forums for our users to share their stories. It's these stories that provide the narrative to strongly engage our communities to invest in their own success.

Libraries play an essential, nonpartisan role in providing the information that allows citizens to make informed decisions. Libraries make a difference. Libraries transform lives. Let's never forget that. Let's speak up.

SELECTED (MOSTLY FREE) WEB REFERENCES

Public Libraries

"Dividends: The Value of Public Libraries in Canada," http://www.cla.ca/divisions/capl/dividends.htm.

"OCLC Community Advocacy and Awareness Site," http://www.oclc.org/advocacy/default.htm.

"Libraries: How They Stack Up" (OCLC),
http://www.oclc.org/reports/2003libsstackup.htm.

"The Public Library: A National Survey,"
http://www.nyla.org/index.php?page_id=801.

"Placing a Value on Public Library Services,"
http://www.slpl.lib.mo.us/libsrc/resresul.htm.

"Public Library Benefits Valuation Study Methodology and Key Findings,"
http://www.slpl.lib.mo.us/using/valuationc.htm; and
http://www.slpl.lib.mo.us/using/valuationg.htm.

"The Role of Public Libraries in Local Economic Development,"
http://www.ku.edu/pri/resrep/pdf/m260.pdf.

"Enhancing Economic Development through Libraries,"
http://www.iira.org/pubsnew/publications/IIRA_Reports_18.pdf.

"National Arts and Economic Prosperity Impact Study: Executive Summary,"
http://www.ci.pasadena.ca.us/planning/arts/Documents/
ecoimpactstudy.pdf.

"Panel on Measuring the Value of Library Services,"
http://www.nclis.gov/libraries/foru96-2.html.

"Making Book: Gambling on the Future of Our Libraries" (Kansas City),
http://www.haplr-index.com/Making%20Book%20KCConsensus
%20Library%20report-execsum.pdf.

"South Carolina Public Library Impact Study,"
http://www.libsci.sc.edu/SCEIS/home.htm.

"Taxpayer Return on Investment in Florida Public Libraries,"
http://dlis.dos.state.fl.us/bld/roi/pdfs/ROISummaryReport.pdf.

"St. Louis Public Library: Placing a Value on Public Library Services,"
http://www.slpl.lib.mo.us/libsrc/rescbec.htm.

"Impacts of the Pennsylvania Nonprofit Sector,"
http://www.pano.org/economic%20impact%20study.pdf.

"British Library: Measuring Our Value,"
http://www.bl.uk/cgi-bin/press.cgi?story=1399; and
http://www.bl.uk/pdf/measuring.pdf.

Academic Libraries

Scott Bennett, "Libraries Designed for Learning,"
http://www.clir.org/pubs/reports/pub122/pub122web.pdf.

"Dimensions and Use of the Scholarly Information Environment,"
http://www.diglib.org/use/grantpub.pdf.

"OCLC White Paper on the Information Habits of College Students,"
http://www5.oclc.org/downloads/community/informationhabits.pdf.

Pew Internet and American Life Project,
http://www.pewinternet.org.

"The Economic Impact of Public Universities,"
http://www.nasulgc.org/publications/EconImpact.pdf.

"The Economic Impact of Higher Education,"
http://www.commonwealthnorth.org/uastudy/pitneyecon.html.

School Libraries

Ken Haycock, "The Crisis in Canada's School Libraries: The Case for Reform
and Reinvestment," Canadian Coalition for School Libraries, 2003,
http://www.peopleforeducation.com/librarycoalition/.

Keith Curry Lance and David V. Loertscher, *Powering Achievement,* 2nd ed.
(Salt Lake City, UT: Hi Willow Research and Publishing, 2003).

Special Libraries

Joanne Gard Marshall's studies on the impact of special libraries:
"The Impact of the Hospital Library on Clinical Decision-Making:
The Rochester Study," http://www.pubmedcentral.gov/articlerender
.fcgi?tool=pmcentrez&artid=225641.
"Patient Education and Health Outcomes: Implications for Library Service,"
http://www.pubmedcentral.gov/articlerender.fcgi?tool=pmcentrez
&artid=227189; and
http://www.sla.org/Presentations/sldc/joanne_LAB2002pp
.ppt#310,25,References.

Joanne G. Marshall, *The Impact of the Special Library on Corporate Decision-
Making* (Washington, DC: Special Libraries Association, 1993).

Statistics

"Normative Data Project for Libraries,"
http://www.librarynormativedata.info.

"NCLIS Statistics and Surveys,"
http://www.nclis.gov/survey.htm.

NCES: National Center for Education Statistics, http://nces.ed.gov.

"Canada: National Core Library Statistics Program,"
http://www.collectionscanada.ca/8/3/r3-203-e.html.

"Canadian Libraries: Bibliography,"
http://www.collectionscanada.ca/8/3/r3-800-e.html.

"ARL Statistics and Measurement Program,"
http://www.arl.org/stats/.

"ALA Office for Research and Statistics,"
http://www.ala.org/ala/ors/statsaboutlib/statisticsabout.htm;
http://www.ala.org/ala/alalibrary/libraryfactsheet/Default1446.htm;
and http://www.ala.org/ala/ors/researchstatistics.htm.

"Library Research Service: Research and Statistics about Libraries,"
http://www.lrs.org.

Other

Ian McCallum and Sherrey Quinn, "Valuing Libraries," *Australian Library Journal* 53, no. 1 (February 2004): 55–69, http://www.alia.org.au/publishing/alj/53.1/full.text/mccallum.quinn.html.

Many of the excerpts in this book come from Abram's blog, *Stephen's Lighthouse*. When he started it in July 2005, he explained his choice of title like this: "The lighthouse theme is based on what lighthouses do—shine a light on the waters and/or sound a horn to help ships navigate the course. They don't always stop the ships from crashing onto the rocks, but they help most of the time" (http://stephenslighthouse.sirsi.com/archives/2005/07/wellcome_to_the.html).

Information Wants to Be Free: Bullcookies

Our work and value have been attacked on many levels, but nothing has been more damaging than the misquote of Stewart Brand that "information wants to be free!" This phrase has served as a clarion call to devalue information, information work, and librarianship which are anything but free.

Here's the real quote. At the first Hackers' Conference in 1984, Brand put his finger on a central paradox about digital information that is causing us so much trouble today. "On the one hand," Brand said, "information wants to be expensive, because it's so valuable. The right information in the right place just changes your life. On the other hand, information wants to be free because the cost of getting it out is getting lower and lower all the time. So you have these two fighting against each other."

"Aha!!!" I said to myself as I read this in David Bollier's book (not free) on a plane (not free) on my way to a conference (not free). There it is. It's just like that old misquote: "Those who don't know history are doomed to repeat it." What Santayana actually wrote in *Reason in Common Sense* was, "Those who forget the past are condemned to repeat it." As Voltaire said, "Common sense is not so common." Why is this quote so compelling—even as a misquote—and why did it get such currency in the modern age? Remember that a hackers' conference in 1984 was pretty much on-the-edge.

Free means many things. It is especially vital to the practice of librarianship. This quote is lifted from page 120 of David Bollier's must-read book, *Silent Theft: The Private Plunder of Our Common Wealth* (Routledge, 2003).

First published in *Stephen's Lighthouse*, August 31, 2005 (http://stephenslighthouse.sirsi.com/archives/2005/08/information_wan_1.html).

Bollier lifted it from [Stewart Brand's report on the Hackers' Conference published in] the *Whole Earth Review,* May 1985, p. 49. You can also see a history of this quote's attribution at "Information Wants to Be Free" at http://www.anu.edu.au/people/Roger.Clarke/II/IWtbF.html.

Free in its narrowest meaning can mean *without cost.* And often from the user's perspective, library services are without cost. More important, it means freedom to think, freedom to research, freedom to write, freedom of expression—those values central to our professional beliefs. *Free* can also mean a kind of shorthand for democracy and democratic principles. The democratization of information has been a movement since at least the invention of the printing press and publishing. *Free* can be used in the context of free time: freedom from obligation, duties, and responsibilities. Libraries' recreational collections certainly fall into this "free" space. Finally, *free* can mean unconstrained running free, thinking free, having the free rights of citizenship. Making information free is very powerful because of all those other meanings. If there's anyone who knows that information wants to be expensive, it has to be librarians. We manage this to ensure cost-effectiveness.

UNFETTERED

My opinion is that the best meaning of *free* is *unfettered.* There are many ways to unfetter information and even more ways to fetter it. Cost is only one of the ways in which we can deal with the fettering of information. By buying information at the enterprise level in our organizations, we unfetter it and make it free, de facto, to the end user. It isn't free of cost by any means, but it will appear free to the user. Therefore, the user does not need to leap the hurdle that is the "buy" decision to use critical information that can underpin his or her work.

We can also fetter information by making it costly or adding hurdles of payments to obtain the information transaction we want. Sometimes fettering information with a cost improves the end-user experience: free movies can be overcrowded, free information can be rough and poorly edited, free can cause quality lapses because you get what you pay for. Therefore, some users prefer to pay to get the assurance of a better information experience and to remove the risk of additional processing fetters.

So in what other ways is information unfettered? Libraries unfetter information—they make it flow freely by the following methods.

Good Information Design

Increasing simplicity and assuring use of good interface principles make the acquisition of information more satisfying. If we don't simplify it, it can be pretty rough. We can all name information systems that were abusive—some of the first-generation Boolean online systems were far too complex to teach to typical end users.

Making It Easier to Find

Users hate to search like us; they just want to find. By using simple tools like federated search and adopting appropriate standards like Z39.50 and SRW, we make life for users much easier. Federated search removes the barrier to not knowing where to search in the first place. And especially by adopting tools like link resolvers that employ the OpenURL standard, we make exploring the information ocean seamless when content is identified and full-text links become simple and seamless.

Pruning Information

Our collection development and content identification skills are nonpareil. Our adherence to selecting high-quality information to meet our users' real needs and to avoid duplication, false paths, and false drops generates real value. Just searching the groups of content that match the domain I am searching is very powerful.

Aligning Information with User Profiles

Again, through great selection we ensure that the information is appropriate for our users—we don't provide jargon-laden information to kids and neophytes when plain language is needed. We design our websites, portals, and learning objects to align with our users' literacy, subject, and learning needs and styles.

Targeting Information to Specific User Communities

We can push information. We know (mostly) how not to drown our folks. We have a fine editor's and selector's eye. We push information intelligently and can use the latest styles of alerts, RSS, and blogs—and still write a powerful paper note or e-mail to alert our users to special items.

Customizing Information to Individual Needs and Projects

Our best feature is that we can improve the quality of a question before we seek an answer. This is the personal research touch that is based in deep knowledge of the reference interview. Search engines seek answers in haste. As the saying goes, haste makes waste and is, by definition, shallow. How shallow can it be to decide quality by just popularity? How high school! What an opportunity for virtual reference services!

REMOVING BARRIERS TO INFORMATION

We know that increasing required actions between the user and content reduces satisfaction and productivity. Therefore, we have become experts in reducing non-value-added barriers. We know that IP authentication can make a seamless experience of paid content. We know that we can remove barriers by avoiding digital rights management or copyright fees. We can assure legal access through invisible patron-level authentication systems, too.

Many of us are challenged by management, users, and researchers who love the Google experience. Google has unfettered access for them on many levels. It's free—*Not.* Advertisers pay for it, and the advertisers are Google's primary clients, not the searcher. A good searcher experience that delivers high numbers of visits and searches—of the right type—generates more ads and therefore more Google revenue.

We likely do need to give unto Google what is Google's. Google gives an amazingly good experience in four of the five "W" questions: who, what, where, and when. We know this as well as end users. What libraries and librarians do better is with questions that start with why and how. When our collections and skills revolve around a central theme, industry, topic, or exploration, we excel at answering and building users' and learners' knowledge in the why and the how. That's why we find libraries represented so strongly in sectors where innovation and creativity are central to success—research and development, universities, advertising, consulting, and auditing, for example.

Libraries and librarians unfetter information in many ways. By doing so we improve the user experience, improve learning, improve knowledge acquisition, and inform decision making. We need to stop worrying about Google competition, since it doesn't even begin to compete with us on a core level. We must start differentiating library services from weak experiences like Google.

In the wisdom that is an e-mail signature, I once read (and can't find the first author of) this quote: "Those who know how will always be employed. They will be working for those who know why."[*]

---

[*] Charles Beaman, West Jessamine High School, Nicholasville, Kentucky, often ended his e-mails with this quote. —Eds.

Abram frequently reminds librarians that they often underestimate their potential influence.

How Many Clicks?

Online visits to Wal-Mart (4.85 percent of net traffic) last Friday passed those to Amazon (2.80 percent of net traffic). Now, I really wonder if we combined all the visits to library websites, where would libraries rank?

According to an old OCLC report ("Libraries: How They Stack Up"), FedEx sends about 5.3 million parcels daily, compared to libraries circulating about 5.4 million items and another 5.7 million online items a day—just about double. Amazon did about 1.5 million items a day. We estimate that SirsiDynix software handles about 2 million items a day.

In the United States there are about 1.1 billion visitors a year [to libraries]—about nine times the number of major sports attendees (about 200 million) in the country. SirsiDynix estimates that about 250 million folks see our software in libraries.

Globally, there are about six times more people with library cards than drivers' licenses! SirsiDynix software manages more patron records than there are drivers' licenses globally.

The number of library locations vastly outnumbers McDonald's and Starbucks combined.

It feels to me like we vastly underestimate our community power and influence. We also underestimate the talent and complex thinking needed to manage this "presence." Maybe we need to craft a better communication of our role and complexity. . . .

First published in *Stephen's Lighthouse,* November 29, 2005 (http://stephenslighthouse .sirsi.com/archives/2005/11/how_many_clicks.html).

It's hard to describe one of Abram's presentations,
but Hane does a good job.

Libraries Can Fight Back

Paula J. Hane

A visionary and funny man, Stephen Abram first set the scenario with all
the things that Google's announced lately and its *many* initiatives—scary
stuff! The company has bought six social networking companies. We let
them read our e-mail and tell us what we want. Soon Google will control
all the ads, all the wallets, all the broadband, etc. . . . So, in the closing keynote for the event, he provided his Top Ten Strategies for competing with
Google. Sage advice in my book.

1. Know your market. He mentioned the Normative Data Project that
   aids market understanding. Know what's circulating. Understand
   geographic use.

2. Know your customers better than Google—or you'll lose. He
   mentioned the "Personas" project that helps in understanding the
   needs, preferences, and desires of users. Check out the article in
   the latest *Computers in Libraries.* Educate yourself on the charac-
   teristics of "Millennials" ("They can think rings around us") and
   also other populations, like older folks. Google does "satisficing"
   where librarians meet Real Needs. Be where your customers are.
   How much of your usage is in person? What about IM (instant
   messaging)?

This brief article, "Libraries Can Fight Back," by Paula J. Hane, is a capsule summary
of Abram's keynote presentation at the "Internet Librarian 2005" conference. The
article first appeared on the *Internet Librarian 2005 Blog* on October 27, 2005, and was
published by Information Today, Inc. (http://www.infotoday.com). Reprinted with
permission. All rights reserved.

3. Searching for the target. . . . Federated search should not look like Google. Build compelling content—in *context*!!!

4. Support your culture. Get your texthead to "nexthead." Move beyond vinyl recordings. Adapt to video and streaming media. Podcasting. Start learning now!

5. Position libraries where we excel. Google does who, what, where, and when questions really well. Google sucks at how and why questions. Libraries' core competency is not the delivery of information. Libraries improve the quality of the question. The question is what's important. Libraries are an "exploration space," not a collection space.

6. Be wireless. The next massive wave of innovation will start in 2006–2007.

7. Get visual. Explore visualization technologies, like Grokker. (Most librarians are text-based learners, and it takes us longer.)

8. Integrate. Build community context first—learning, research, neighborhood, workplace, culture/entertainment.

9. For Pete's sake, take a risk.

10. And his last—focus.

We, as librarians, have to learn that when we study something to death, death was not our original goal. Pick something, do it well, and move on.

In the next few articles, Abram directly challenges
librarians to be more vocal in their advocacy efforts.

The Challenge Ahead—Sustaining Our Relevance

We have seen, in the past few months (I am writing this in November 2003), extreme advances in the area of interoperability, especially on the desktop. The lines are really blurring—between content and context, between software and hardware, between wired and wireless, between entertainment and work. Indeed, the new Millennials, that generation the first of whom are just now finishing their bachelor's degrees, are coming into a world that's beautifully designed to match their learning and information-seeking behaviors. It might just leave us behind too—groan—if we don't think smart and work quickly and nimbly to ensure special librarians' continued relevance.

Well folks, I think that there are some real threats and opportunities for us here. We survived the data revolution. We helped lead the information revolution. We coped and are coping with the knowledge economy. This last shift, though, is the toughest. We are actually starting to see the seamless integration of information and content into the working, learning, playing, and entertainment environments of our users. Instead of just helping people become more knowledgeable with our service, we will be contributing to the world of improved human behavior. We certainly can't "own" that, but we can now seriously contemplate the SLA slogan—Turning Information Into Action!

First published in *Information Outlook* 9, no. 1 (January 2004): 20–21. © Special Libraries Association. All rights reserved. Reprinted with permission.

HERE'S THE STRATEGY

Off the top of my head, I can see a few key strategies you must focus on to emerge from this challenge new and improved!

We must communicate the critical role that information literacy skills play in our organizations. While the role of librarians in training and educating end users in these key skills is obvious, we are not an easily sealed solution. So many users, so little time, and so few of us! We'll need to investigate e-learning, distance learning for bibliographic skills, information coaching (using IM and virtual reference), and ensuring that our students and professional and work colleagues are ready to adapt to this new age. Run—don't walk—down to your human resources vice president and start building a relationship. You need to be mainstream in HR for organization development issues and training.

We also need to inform our executives about "information risk." Let's acknowledge that this isn't just about copyright—although that is a clear financial and management risk. It's also the risk of making decisions based on bad information—and bad information does happen to good people. We have too many stories of companies being hurt, patients getting ill, and manufacturing systems failing owing to blind faith in electronically delivered information. Run—don't walk—down to your corporate counsel or executive vice president in charge of quality and start building a relationship. You need to be connected to the executives who care about this stuff.

As always, we sit in an interesting space. We build our key (and unique) competencies on a deep understanding of content. We need to lift up our eyes and see a new technological, human, and enterprise context. We've always known that it's not about the wiring and the pipelines, it's not about the software, hardware, and applications—and it's definitely not about the desktop. For librarians, it's always been about the people.

Once more, with feeling: knowledge can only exist in people's brains. We help people and organizations of people get smarter.

What Is Your Information Outlook?

Jane I. Dysart and Stephen K. Abram

We stand on the edge of our future—a future celebrated in this inaugural issue of *Information Outlook*. The word *outlook* can be looked at in many different ways, which is particularly important to SLA as we approach the millennium. It's the perfect word to describe the challenges and opportunities facing special librarians and information professionals at the dawn of the Information Era—our era. One of our challenges will be to maintain SLA's relevance through the future.

From one perspective, the word *outlook* means observing, as if from a lookout—rising above the trees and seeing the forest. This means looking out from a panoramic perspective—not at the detail, but at the beauty of the view, the landscape. For us it's more than just a local or national perspective—it's a global view, international in scale. From this vantage point we can create maps, find patterns, prioritize places to explore, communicate the contexts of this new age with others, and help create the new rules for success. As we find our sea legs in this new age, we will need to expand on the core skills and talents necessary for this advanced global network and its cross-cultural context—we need to be linking content and context, developing new communities, and building new connections.

Another aspect of our information outlook is our outlook on life—our attitudes toward our own lives, our profession, and our future. Do we expect success or marginalization? Do we foresee our future as utopia or dystopia? Do we sense the potential to have an impact or not? SLA's vision

First published in *Information Outlook* 1 (January 1997): 34–36. © Special Libraries Association. All rights reserved. Reprinted with permission.

is positive: to be catalysts in the Information Age. In this era, we will no longer be regarded merely as skilled professionals, competent to perform professional information work. We are advancing to the level of true "talent." We are positioned with the four key talents necessary for success in this Information Age—and are probably the only group of professionals so blessed with this full suite of assets:

Our advanced technology skills. We're not saying that we are the keepers of the secrets of hardware, software, or communications. We have something more important to this new age. We understand, at a deep professional level, two things that are more critical—true information applications and the human/information interface. In this age, it is not as important how the technology works, but rather, what you do with it and how easily information can be turned into knowledge. If this transformation of information into knowledge doesn't occur, technology is just spinning its wheels without a true payoff.

Our advanced service professionalism. We are not information servants or seekers of information "McJobs" in the new economy. We are exactly what intelligent enterprises need on their senior teams to effectively use real tools and strategies to lubricate their organizations with information for success.

Our advanced information literacy skills. As professional accountants are to financial health and medical professionals are to personal health, professional librarians are to an organization's information health. As the content tsunami threatens to engulf the enterprise, it becomes essential that our collection, evaluation, research, interpretation, training, and communication skills be applied in the highest level of strategic context.

Our advanced people skills. We sometimes refer to the application of these skills by using our own jargon—the reference interview, library board management, end user training. However, they are nonetheless essential elements in the continuum of content transfer—data becomes information, information becomes knowledge, and knowledge, if we're lucky, becomes wisdom. Each of these transfers and transformations requires people, and people require help. Special librarians can provide that help—either by understanding the information context and designing content products to deliver information effectively, or by helping the end user directly.

Much like the weather outlook provided by a meteorologist, our outlook also tells us what we can expect for the future. Looking into the next hundred years of SLA, we can safely predict nothing and everything. We can foresee an era where the convergence of multiple technologies will result in equally powerful personal and enterprise-wide applications—true information applications, not merely automated information-manufacturing processes. We can foresee new dimensions of service, personal and enterprise-wide, where the lines are blurred between what constitutes a mass market, an information product, a desktop, and an answer. We can certainly see new and different professional and personal relationships. Who would have predicted that many of us now carry on successful relationships, on many levels, with people we've never seen, heard, or met except through the Internet?

We can see that the solutions now emerging regarding networking, hardware, and software provide a context for a new renaissance in information design. Remember that during the last renaissance, it was not standard—by any means—that books be read from left to right, from front to back; that they have covers; or even that they be square! The print paradigm we've dealt with for centuries was the result of years of creative and iterative effort. This is what is happening again in the electronic context. Special librarians can be key players in this effort—many already are. However, we must move from being "textheads" to "nextheads," since this renaissance will encompass more than text—bringing in broadcasting, images, sound, moving images, and animation. It will be a massive convergence never before seen in world history. It is truly exciting to see some of our members moving beyond the development of just-in-case collections and just-in-time research, and into senior roles in enterprise-wide knowledge management.

Our outlook for the future should involve striking a balance among the pillars of our profession. We need to balance the competing needs of users, libraries, institutions, governments, technology, budgets, suppliers, and the public and private sectors, while simultaneously ensuring that we don't stray from our core values as a profession. (Our core values are included in the SLA Vision Statement, which can be found on SLA's home page at http://www.sla.org.)

After years of being on the fringes of intellectual and economic mainstream activity, librarianship now finds itself dead center. We've been put there by developments such as Netscape, AltaVista, Yahoo, artificial intelligence, the World Wide Web and hypertext, Java, and alternative information channels. These are much more than just products and processes; they are true transformational events. When we talk about issues like the intuitiveness of a GUI or an attempt to design cognitive systems that match how we all think, we are tampering with the nature of learning and the basic construction of society. We need to view the panorama of people, citizens, and clients around us—recognizing all of their different outlooks and perspectives. We have the skills. More important, we have an enriched and informed point of view. We have the ability to link with others to successfully deal with these issues and create innovative solutions.

Finally, a librarian's outlook depends on the professional's way of thinking. In regard to technology, the most recognizable strategic lever in this new age, librarians have always been willing to explore a new outlook and way of doing things. Librarians have been early adopters of virtually every major technological innovation of the last hundred years—we used microfilm before spies did, online databases before Dow Jones, CDs before Bruce Springsteen, and the Internet before it captured the imaginations of the mass media and the average consumer. Most others are novices compared to us. We were there in the development of the passing age, biding our time, and contributing in no small measure to past successes.

"Whether or not it is clear to you, no doubt the universe is unfolding as it should" (Max Ehrmann, "Desiderata"). Our challenge is to ensure that we are active participants in shaping this new age. What happens next should happen because we worked on it and contributed to its development. This is our challenge, and the outlook is good.

Post–Information Age Positioning for Special Librarians

Is Knowledge Management the Answer?

> *Knowledge is power, not information. Information is power only if you can take action with it.* —Daniel Burrus[*]

In this article, I will take a few heretical positions that will challenge some of the sacred cows of our profession. Unlike most heretics, though, I will suggest a replacement for these views that I hope will steer us on to a better course to the future of special librarianship and, at the very least, initiate a debate on the best positions for SLA and special librarianship.

HERESY NUMBER ONE
SPECIAL LIBRARIANS ARE NOT IN THE INFORMATION BUSINESS

We, as special librarians, made a potentially disastrous error those many years ago when we decided to position ourselves in the "information business." Information businesses are marked by their ability to create information and disseminate it widely—often for a profit. Generally, special librarians do not, as a part of our core mandate, create information. While we do create information about information (metadata), I believe this is a higher-

First published in *Information Outlook* 1, no. 6 (June 1997): 18–24. © Special Libraries Association. All rights reserved. Reprinted with permission.

[*] Daniel Burrus is one of the world's leading technology forecasters and is the founder and CEO of Burrus Research Associates, Inc., a research and consulting firm that specializes in global innovations in science and technology, their creative application and future impact. —Eds.

level calling in the knowledge continuum. The drive to stake out territory by positioning special librarianship as being in the information business has produced a number of negative behaviors that have, in my opinion, limited our ability to make as much forward progress in our profession as we might desire. Examples of this behavior include the following ones.

The growth of data professionals and technology experts into information roles has been perceived as a threat by many of our members. This has driven behaviors that militate against making a partnership with the very group that has access to the advanced technology and data skills we seek for success. We lose the ability to display our complementary skill set and are forced into a competitive positioning.

We view the natural progression of our traditional partners and supporters—information suppliers and publishers—as a threat, too. Their strategies to access the information end user at the desktop are the next, most logical step for them to survive. Suppliers and publishers must protect and expand their traditional professional end user markets as their old retail, library, and direct mail channels are disintermediated by the Internet and the World Wide Web.

We view the entrance of new players into the information field as a threat. Indeed, we've seen some library associations putting forward position papers to the traditional suppliers asking them to slow the pace of change and adoption of new technologies!

HERESY NUMBER TWO
SPECIAL LIBRARIANS CANNOT MANAGE KNOWLEDGE

Currently, we are running the risk of lurching headlong into a new positioning of our profession and our role as "knowledge managers." The plain fact is that knowledge per se cannot be managed. In fact, capturing knowledge in any form other than into a human being's brain reduces it to mere information, or worse, data. Only the knowledge environment can be managed.

The reality is that special librarians—possibly all librarians—have operated at a level superior to mere knowledge management. We play a role in the knowledge "environment" as key catalysts in the knowledge continuum. Information systems technology professionals will have grown from their data roots into information management and the systems to support information—including delivery, integration, search interfaces, etc. Our success as a profession has historically been where we are associated with knowledge-based enterprises (universities, media, engineering, accounting, consulting firms, etc.) or with the knowledge-intensive portions of corporations (research and development, sales and marketing, strategic planning, etc.). This is primarily because our contribution to the knowledge environment of our organizations is a tangible one directly related to successful decision making.

WHAT ARE THE KEYS TO SUCCESSFUL TRANSFORMATIONAL LIBRARIANSHIP?

The keys to our future success lie in the following strategies.

1. Focusing on Where the Transformations Occur

Instead of thinking of our professional skills as being informational skills, we should look at what we do as transformational. Sometimes this is called "adding value." But most of the time our added value is in the transformation, and not in the products and tools we use. When we organize information, we are taking data, books, and bookmark files and making them more accessible and useful to the end user. When we create indexes and catalogs, we are creating tools and services to ensure less time is spent in the hunt for information and more time is available to turn it into knowledge. Indeed, these skills have now become so important they have been renamed "metadata" skills or competencies in the development of information about information. One has only to search AltaVista a few times and get 200,000 hits to powerfully understand the importance of metadata skills to the knowledge economy!

2. Focusing on the Learning Organization

The key activity that happens when users interact with us, our libraries, and our services is "learning." Organizations that encourage learning and focus on learning in its broadest context will, I believe, be all the more successful. Strategist Peter M. Senge's works—including the book *The Fifth Discipline: The Art and Practice of the Learning Organization*—contain many methods and theories for developing learning organizations.

3. Turning Information into Knowledge and Putting Knowledge to Work

Here is perhaps the biggest opportunity for us as special librarians. We have no primary need to look backward and see the growth of emerging professions into the information world. We must look forward into the knowledge economy and carve out a strategic niche for ourselves that allows our profession to have an impact in the new economy. The role for us in the new world is to be the guides and navigators for the exploration of the information ocean. We must develop new services and products while enhancing our skills to underpin meaningful social and economic development. Remember the three "I's": we will form the base for informed, intelligent, and impactful decision making in our society and enterprises. Special librarianship will be one of the catalysts in this development—if we focus our skills, knowledge, and energies in this direction.

4. Learning the Tools of Transformational Librarianship

We know technology is vitally important to the emerging knowledge economy. We will *never* forget that technology is just a tool, an enabler to the creation of the new age, a focus for opportunity, and not the driver of change. The drivers of change are the people who adopt the enabling technologies and use them to promote improvements to knowledge creation and the management of the knowledge environment.

CONCLUSION

The Information Age ended sometime in 1995. It was an abject failure—not because information wasn't hugely important, but because the society of the old era continued to view and measure the Information Age with tools, paradigms, and strategies suited to that time. It's fascinating to watch the economists for the old economy furiously trying to apply supply and demand models to the information economy! Especially since supply and demand economics presumes a limited supply of something, and that success accrues to those who harness the limited supply for wealth creation. Information, of course, is in unlimited supply, and the emergence of the commercial Internet and the World Wide Web in 1995 destroyed an age! Future success will not go to those enterprises that corner or manage limited supplies or serve a manageable demand, but to those enterprises and professions that can effectively manage this unlimited supply of key and vital information through filtering, organizing, and improving accessibility.

TAKING THE KNOWLEDGE POSITION

My belief about using the knowledge environment as the paradigm for viewing our professional challenges at the dawn of this new age causes me to ask four key questions:

1. By moving toward information aimed at the needs of an individual as opposed to a group, do the role and importance of large databases aimed at mass markets decline?

2. Does increasing the number of information transactions make an organization more successful? Or should we focus on the quality of the transaction?

3. If we accept that knowledge can only be stored effectively in an individual human brain, how do we store data and provide services so that information can be absorbed as knowledge faster?

4. What are the roles of special librarians in having material and measurable impacts on the behaviors within their organizations or upon their clients?

Largely because it continues to be useful in understanding the changes that our society is undergoing, we still see the popular press trumpeting the arrival of an Information Age—an era that ended years ago. We know better—and we have the skills, in alliance with information technology professionals and emerging or traditional information businesses, to transform our enterprises in preparation for enormous success. Grasping the opportunity now to position ourselves and our organizations for the knowledge-based economy is vital. As part of this repositioning, I propose we think seriously about taking the knowledge positioning for SLA in support of its members.

Although all thirty-two tips in Abram's article are good, we've only included a few in this excerpt.

Thirty-Two Tips to Inspire Innovation for You and Your Library

There's nothing like your twenty-fifth anniversary since graduating from library school to cause you to reflect. What have I learned in those twenty-five years, and is any of it useful? Each of these points below has at least one story underpinning the learning—and usually many. As I wrote this column, I was surprised by how many little rules and insights drive my perceptions of innovation and product development. Hence, this column mushroomed into a three-parter. And, as I find to always be the case, there was some pain and some gain associated with learning these insights. I can't guarantee that each philosophy will work as well for you as they do for me (or as the kids say, YMMV—Your Mileage May Vary) or in every situation. Also, when I look them over I see that some are attitudes more than aptitudes. That's interesting to me. Attitude is everything. When you're positive, positive things happen. Anyway, I have collected this list over a few years and thought that I would share it with you this summer. So here goes.

2. GOOD NOT PERFECT

This is one that many of us have difficulty dealing with. We are, after all, a profession that covets the perfect catalog record, believes that we can orga-

First published in *SirsiDynix OneSource,* July 5, 2005 (part 1); August 3, 2005 (part 2); and October 26, 2005 (part 3) (http://www.imakenews.com/sirsi/e_article000423643 .cfm; http://www.imakenews.com/sirsi/e_article000436456.cfm; http://www .imakenews.com/sirsi/e_article000458643.cfm).

nize all of the world's knowledge for universal access, *and* sits behind desks offering to answer all comers' questions. Pretty nervy! It is a challenge for us to know when to release new products and services and when to decide something is done, finished, and complete. Perfection as an attitude gets in the way of this decision. When our stock-in-trade was mostly uncorrectable hard copy, this served us well. Now that we spend so much time in designing malleable interfaces, web products, and content that is correctable and improvable on the fly, we need to decide when good enough is good enough. A valued colleague used to quote this "Good Not Perfect" aphorism in so many meetings that we bought her a T-shirt. This maxim broke the perfectionist mind-set logjam so often, and we all benefited from the real learning derived from working with the real product instead of the product in our minds.

3. IT'S NOT THE NUMBER OF STEPS THAT CAUSES DELAYS IN DEVELOPMENT—IT'S THE SPACE BETWEEN THE STEPS

Have you ever been frustrated with how long it takes to accomplish projects? Of course you have. I have noticed that it's not the number of steps in your project plan that determines how long the project takes. It's when you take a breather between every step that causes delays. Now, I am not saying that rushing is good, but good project management minimizes the space between the steps and stays focused on achieving the milestones and ultimate goal. I know that many websites benefit from regularly scheduled updates and improvements. Others seem to stay static and fossilized for years until they require complete removal and rebuilding. By sticking to a pattern of innovation and improvement, things stay dynamic and engaging.

5. PREFER ACTION OVER STUDY

If you or your team is studying something to death—remember that death was not the original goal! I have been in libraries where their systems folks in the host institution were studying whether to upgrade from Windows 95 to 98 in 2005! Scary. Although we have a great core competency in research and study, we must know when to fish or cut bait. In risk-averse cultures this is particularly difficult. What needs to be learned and understood is that delay is as big a risk as poorly considered action. Pilots and good processes reduce your risk (and provide learning opportunities too). This philosophy is closely related to the one where an enterprise values its conservative culture and gradually declines due to its lack of adaptation to modern expectations.

6. BRAINSTORM, MOCK-UP, BUILD, ALPHA, REBUILD, BETA, PILOT, TEST, LAUNCH, EVALUATE, REDO

And there's the process. It's pretty simple, and many make the mistake of trying to skip a step. I've rarely seen a skipped step that didn't cause problems later. Each step can be quite small and contained. You don't need to bet the organization's future on a single initiative—writ large in the strategic plan. You do need to actively seek to have many projects at different stages of development in your funnel. That way you have built innovation processes into the DNA of your culture. By building teams focused on a few key initiatives—for example, virtual reference, Rooms, and web portals—you can focus attention and run several projects in parallel. This starts to create excitement and a practical image of action over study.

8. REMEMBER THE 15 PERCENT RULE

Humans have extreme difficulty in actually seeing a comparative difference of less than 15 percent. I once read that research shows that when we see the light from 100 candles, we don't see a difference in brightness until 115 candles are lit. Interesting. I understand that the same thing is true of sound volume, color variation, and other matters of human perception. Indeed, in job evaluation systems, jobs are not considered sufficiently different until there is a 12.5–15 percent difference in the jobs' points. So what I have learned here is that innovation needs to be sufficiently different from what was there before for humans (users) to see the difference. Some people think that making 100 things 2 percent better will make a perceptible difference. This isn't likely true, and for our purposes, we should probably attempt to make a much smaller group of initiatives 15 percent or more better. I also think that this is why single, small introductions of new features on library portals are often missed or ignored until they're pointed out. They're not sufficiently different to be perceived and noticed. Therefore, it might be better to make grander changes to bring attention to new services and products in our virtual space.

12. GET OUT OF YOUR BOX!

It is unlikely that you are the alpha user profile. Understand that. I know that as a librarian I am pretty limited in my ability to really connect with the challenges faced by newbie library, web, or database searchers. I am not saying that I can't overcome this, but I have to be explicitly aware that my training, biases, and experiences have forever changed me and my perceptions of the information world. It also means that when I am designing services for seniors, kids, teens, challenged communities, the "differently-abled," or even other professions like lawyers or engineers, I have to keep in mind that I need to be aware of and prioritize their needs and competencies over my own. I find that it pays to remind myself that I am not trying to create products and services for mini-librarians—and that this is a poor goal in the first place. I need to understand the user's context and needs and not project my own onto them. For instance, it is likely that the end user doesn't actually want "information" but, more likely, wants to be informed, entertained, taught, and/or transformed in some manner. Libraries are great environments for that.

13. "PRODUCTIZE"

Be able to physically point to your product or service. It's a problem that so many library products and services are intangible. Until we can name them and point to them as if they were a tangible service or product, they will be undervalued and underappreciated by our users. It will also be difficult for our supporters to articulate what it is that truly makes their library experience transformational. For instance, branding your service and tying your name and institution to the brand is essential. Look at how much more successful library OPACs and websites for teens and kids are when they are associated with a strong branding program and marketing plan. I love the special branding that some of SirsiDynix's clients have put on their catalogs and websites. Also, learn how much more articulate we are about our traditional services when a new element arrives. For example, traditional reference work has described itself much better since virtual reference and instant messaging reference services were introduced. It focused the mind on what value was being delivered and the individual strengths of face-to-face and virtual reference services. The Amazon.com book suggestion features challenged reader advisory services to stretch (and helped us to develop the SirsiDynix Reading Rooms), and the impact of Google on professional database searching needs no illustration.

15. REMEMBER FABS (FEATURES VS. BENEFITS)

Understand the differences between features, functions, and benefits. It's easy to design hundreds of features and functions into a product or service. It is hard to know which ones are the most important to each user. The true skill is in knowing what the benefit of each is. Who is deriving the benefit: The end user? The administration? The intermediary? The vendor? Identifying who derives the ultimate benefit helps you decide who wants your product or service. If it doesn't meet someone's true need, then seriously question whether it's worth doing. It should also meet the need of your priority target user. Then you must market and sell the benefits to your users—not the features and functions. Imagine an ATM at the bank that was marketed as buttons that told you your bank balance—instead of as a convenience!

16. DON'T ASSUME—TEST

You may believe that you understand your customer. You may even have been a customer or "ordinary" person or "normal" user in a past life. You may think that you know what the user will do in nearly every situation. Don't believe it. There is nothing more humbling than discovering the infinite variety of user paths, behaviors, and thinking patterns out there in the real world. It's a bowl of gourmet jelly beans with a few M&Ms thrown in for good measure! Chant this mantra: "I will test my assumptions; I will test my assumptions." It's better to be humbled in your beta test than embarrassed in the marketplace.

17. OBSERVE

Don't just ask your clients what they do, will do, or want. *Observe* them. It has been my observation that users can't, won't, or don't tell you what they are really doing online or on the Web. When I watch them, I see all sorts of user behaviors that are interesting and useful. Some theorists claim that retrospective coherence (or the ability to make sense of something after the fact) causes this contradiction. Also, users just can't imagine how much better something can be. They only want to satisfy a need and get frustrated when there are barriers to that satisfaction. By watching their real behaviors (and sometimes using keystroke trackers or cams), we see where that frustration occurs and can start to think more creatively about ways to improve that website or search experience.

18. HAVE A VISION AND DREAM BIG!

At SirsiDynix, we try to be future focused. We know that we can't build the future without you and your ideas and energy. I have seen the power of vision in every workplace I have been employed in. When it is absent, the workplace is missing something and verges on the horrible. When a shared vision is present, we have achieved great things. When the vision doesn't have enough stretch in it, things seem mediocre. Think back to great work environments you've worked in or great leaders you've worked for, and you'll usually find that there were some great and compelling visions at work there. And for those who don't dream big and have a vision, they're doomed to an endless series of the present. I hope they love the way things are.

19. ASK THE THREE MAGIC QUESTIONS

What keeps you awake at night? If you could solve only one problem at work, what would it be? If you could change one thing and one thing only, what would it be?

I have discovered that these questions are truly magic. They start conversations with users rather than delivering simple answers. They're open-ended instead of closed-ended, yes or no answer questions. Just set the context and ask away. I have used these questions with primary school kids, titans of industry like Bill Gates, librarians, IT managers, and cabinet ministers. These questions work every time to delve deeply into our users' needs and personal goals. When we are armed with that knowledge, then our libraries are unstoppable.

20. NEVER UNDERESTIMATE THE CUSTOMER

Our customers (users, clients, learners, et al.) come with an infinite range of skills and abilities. While we may strive for simple, we have to avoid being simplistic. Never shoot to please the lowest common denominator. That strategy ensures that you'll displease the widest range of users. For example, some love the spare Google interface with loads of white space. It is clean and spare. It also forces users to find the information density and deeper information they need elsewhere. The most popular websites our users use (CNN, CBC Newsworld, *USA Today,* etc.) are deftly dense, and people survive fine. Users have demonstrated an amazing elasticity to adopt complex solutions to their information and life problems. We can't force too much on them at once, but we shouldn't ascribe this learning curve to an inability to adapt—it just takes time. SirsiDynix's Enterprise Portal Solution takes advantage of our users' ability to handle a great deal more information on a screen and to provide more context and content at the same time. The public is ready for more density.

21. SEEK THE REAL CUSTOMER

This is harder than it sounds. There are always important stakeholders in any product. For example, a simple website for students can involve teachers, administrators, IT folks, librarians, content creators, parents, curriculum developers, and, just by the way, the kid. Whose needs must absolutely be met, and whose needs take second seat? It's a very hard question, and I've seen development teams have serious debates arguing for one focus over another. Either way, make sure you meet the needs of the real end user. Many a product has failed by meeting the needs of the wrong population. (Just ask yourself the simple question for each feature and function—"Who cares?" Perhaps a simple example: "If I add DRM to this product—Who cares?" The end user? Administrators? The content provider? Hmmm.) SirsiDynix Rooms needs to be built for the ultimate end user, while the SirsiDynix Rooms Builder needs to be optimized for the librarian, professor, or curriculum leader who is actually building the content.

22. RESPECT DIVERSITY

There's an enormous amount of diversity out there, and it is not just traditional diversity around income, gender, sexual orientation, race, culture, ethnicity, or language. Of particular interest to information professionals is diversity of information literacy skills, learning styles, and multiple intelligences. There is a significant body of research in the education and library sciences that should be understood here. That's where the research is being done about understanding persons and not just technology! I have found that spending time learning from the works of Bloom, Gardner, and Piaget in the fields of learning and intelligence pays off richly in better understanding of user behaviors.

25. BRING MANAGEMENT ON BOARD FIRST

Then add customers and users, *before* you launch. This is a truism in every book about innovation and product management. Yet it is shocking how often it's ignored. Without your management on board, and understanding the goals, product, and overall agenda, you risk failure. They are a key stakeholder and can certainly drive a stake through the heart of your project. Keep them in the loop, continuously.

26. FEEDBACK IS A GIFT

Like that wedding gift from Aunt Sally, you can keep it, display it, return it, or hide it in the closet. It's your choice. Don't overvalue one piece of out-of-context feedback or let it loom out of perspective and balance. Feedback is best digested in the aggregate rather than in small doses. Squeaky wheels are fine and need to be oiled. But if it's the engine that needs attention, then that well-oiled wheel is just a distraction. Feedback shouldn't be cause for stomach-wrenching stress. You are in control of how it can be dealt with (good or constructive or bad) and need to hear and accept this gift from your stakeholders. Do you have feedback mechanisms on your website?

27. MEASURE—DON'T JUST COUNT

Decision makers *cannot* interpret your statistics. They either don't have enough background or just don't have the time to invest. You have to do it for them. This is the real beauty of the Normative Data Project. It allows you to compare numbers between like library systems and branches. SirsiDynix's Director's Station lets you find insights into the basic operating information of your library. Between the NDP and Director's Station you have the power of Wal-Mart-style systems at your own fingertips. Wal-Mart knows what goods are selling every day and to whom. They know exactly where their customers live and everything about the nature of the neighborhoods and communities they are serving. The census, the National Center for Education Statistics data, maps, and library-use information in the NDP or tracked in your Director's Station data and Unicorn reports are great data and are made infinitely easier to use and more timely through SirsiDynix's products. You can be as smart as a Fortune Top 50 corporation! The ability from both NDP and Director's Station to create perfect visuals (bar charts, pie charts, graphs, and maps) that communicate difficult financial and statistical information effectively to decision makers is great.

29. CHEAP IS EXPENSIVE

Especially in the long run—think of cheap products as pilots for the real implementation. This seems obvious, but I am always shocked by the needless nickel-and-diming that limits the success of a project. Good budgeting and management are truly necessary, but financing success is different and means having a value system that sets doing it right as a priority rather than doing it cheap as a best practice. Every real project should recognize the real costs in conversions, customization, user adoption, marketing, introduction, launch, and client support, etc.

30. BUILD FOR THE FUTURE

Too often projects that are planned for 18–36 months naively assume that things will stay the same technologically. Remember the lessons of the past where things mutated quickly—DOS became Windows, diskettes became CD-ROMs, Netscape begat MSIE which begat Firefox, online dial-up became web broadband, etc. You can't be certain of the future, but you can't wait for total stability either. That's the ambiguity. Dealing with ambiguity is a key competency in change management and introducing innovation.

32. NO MISTAKE IS EVER FINAL

One of my better bosses had this phrase framed on the wall of her office. She said she was going to get it in needlepoint one day. We were part of a skunk works that was tasked with re-technologizing a major corporation, as well as introducing transformational change into a huge market and changing the overall culture of the companies involved. No small task. Not only did we make many mistakes, but we also learned from them. If we weren't making mistakes, we weren't trying hard enough. Albeit, we tried to limit the exposure of our experiments, but like learning to skate, if you're not falling down, you're just not learning well enough. Her sign "No mistake is ever final" encouraged us to try just that little bit harder to achieve greatness because we knew we had her support. If you want to change things for the better, you have to be a change agent, and that means you have to be more comfortable with making mistakes and dealing with them effectively—and learning all the time.

BONUS TIP: HAVE SOME FUN!

We are often too serious. Our work is serious, and our impact on our communities is enormous! However, working creatively, trying new things, and being innovative are fun. Take the time to recognize that and live your life to the fullest. Celebrate your successes and your team's work. Champion your library's achievements! Reward your colleagues when they succeed. Don't ever get so heads-down that you can't see the big picture. It's a wonderful world.

Abram's SLA President-Elect Candidate's Statement to the Leadership Summit

Good afternoon, leaders.

Today, I decided to give you a better understanding of me, my background, and my track record. I bring a great deal of experience with associations, volunteer organizations, teams, and special library management, as well as leadership positions with information suppliers.

WHAT WOULD I WANT TO DO IN MY TIME ON THE SLA BOARD?

1. *Focus.* Number one—If we want our profession to achieve something great, then we have to do it with a laserlike focus and dream big. We are a rich, intelligent, diverse, and multihued profession and have a valid and supportable interest in just about everything. However, my dream is that we discover the will within us to focus on a single major mega-project that will benefit us all during my term.

2. *Recognition.* Libraries radiate throughout the knowledge ecology and make a difference. I'd like more decision makers to notice this! Let's work on getting someone who values us to be a highly visible champion. We need to move beyond ourselves and develop and *implement an advocacy program about the role, value, and impact of special librarians and information professionals.* If we fail at this one thing, we do risk losing everything altogether.

3. *Confidence.* Let's find the confidence to speak as a profession with authority, confidence, and energy. Let's do this now. Now! Let's not study

First published in *Information Outlook* 10, no. 4 (April 2006): 8–10. © Special Libraries Association. All rights reserved. Reprinted with permission.

it loooonnnggg and haaarrrddd. Let's not take it literally and study something to death. The death of our profession isn't our goal!! We need to have the confidence of our convictions and take action—sustainable action. If members positioned themselves to each tell just five positive springboard stories in 2006 to five people who matter, our world *would* change. Fifty-thousand stories will move minds. Imagine if SLA focused on supporting its members even more strongly in our efforts!

4. *Balance.* Let's balance all of the needs of every type of specialized librarianship. Our differences are small and our common needs are great. Let's find the middle ground that lets us work more strongly together. We're all in this boat together, and no one part of special librarianship can point to another and say their side of the boat is sinking. Let's sacrifice our pedantic conversations about our titles, our profession's name, how relevant we are. Talking among ourselves is just sound and fury.

5. *Trust and respect.* We need to respect each other more. We need to build better teams and more sustainable effort. We are a smart profession with strong critical thinking skills. We need to ensure that we don't devolve that critical thinking strength into random criticism. We need to have faith in our cause. We need to be an incubator of success.

6. *Risk.* Let's take this risk. Small risk, small reward. Our need is great; we won't get to where we want and need to be without taking some calculated more sizable risks. As Eugenie Prime hollered at our Seattle conference—*no puny visions!*

WHAT EXPERIENCE DO I HAVE TO ACCOMPLISH THIS?

I am pretty action-oriented. I'd like to talk about some of the key projects that I have been involved in to give you a sense of my style.

As president of the Canadian Library Association, I put together strong teams where we influenced national policy on a macro scale. I had the privilege to lead a large team of librarians in influencing the information agenda in the last two national elections in Canada through a campaign of education and conversation. This campaign was even complimented in the Senate of Canada.

We were successful in enhancing the library book postal rate and building a new partnership with Canada Post. We sought and institutionalized professional advice on our advocacy work and reinvigorated a national training program for library advocacy. Our team also heavily influenced the copyright process in Canada. I helped build a new collaborative initiative around school libraries that changed the national landscape. I am also currently co-chairing a huge team (over fifty librarians) on the 8 Rs that seeks to deal with the next generation of library workers. And I'll be talking more about that at the SLA conference in June.

In the past two years I have visited every Canadian library training program and met with every dean. I also sit on the advisory board of a U.S. library school. Within the context of the 8 Rs we are influencing curriculum and not just talking (dare I say, not whining) about it. As an adjunct professor at the University of Toronto's Faculty of Information Studies, I meet and admire the next generation of library students. We need to build them up and engage them aggressively.

Also, at CLA we built a new style of conference planning team that focused on the *strategic* needs of Canadian librarians in the global context and built new delegate-focused tracks on advocacy, leadership, and technology that were a huge success.

As president of the Ontario Library Association (OLA), I made sure that we focused on and made progress on a limited number of strategic projects. We created a long-term team to achieve our vision of a province-wide digital library, called Knowledge Ontario. Our weekly and monthly meetings with the ministries, cabinet, and premier will pay off with a major multimillion-dollar announcement in 2006 building on the over $700,000 in funding so far.

Big visions. Big effort. Huge payoff.

Our OLA team also planned and executed a conference on the crisis in school libraries that generated energy for success and resulted in many new jobs for school librarians during a period of extreme threat—just like some of our SLA members are facing.

Last, we addressed one aspect of diversity in Ontario librarianship and we founded a new and fully financed $300,000 scholarship fund to ensure that a person of native ancestry was in the University of Toronto's library program in perpetuity.

On the international front, I led a team last year that worked cooperatively with the International Federation of Library Associations (IFLA) to raise about $25,000 for tsunami relief and ensured that our membership in IFLA derived value from managing and distributing the funds ethically. As well, I helped my employer do focus groups—*before* the Gulf hurricane tragedies hit—with clients who had dealt with these disasters before. As such, we were prepared to act quickly and sent truckloads of computers and wireless networks to the region right away, along with volunteers and staff. We even bought and equipped a bookmobile in partnership with others to send to the region. I am proud to work as part of these teams.

Sometimes you lead, sometimes you follow, and sometimes you cheer folks on. That's the role of a leader.

Within SLA I have volunteered for about twenty-five years. I have led committees for strategic planning, public relations, and committee on committees and have been a member of many more, including AOOC and finance. I have led my chapter and a division. I have coordinated five major change-oriented task forces for SLA and chaired the branding task force and have chaired or been a member of three others.

In each case, it was the teamwork that made the day and not the contribution of a single person. I have learned a lot and feel proud of our accomplishments.

I care deeply about sharing and networking. These values must be strong in a leader. As evidence of my commitment to share, I point you toward the over 100 articles I wrote this year, including my column for *Information Outlook*. I give over 100 keynote and other speeches a year to library and non-library groups. I have contributed to many books, and will publish another in 2006 through ALA Editions. I also blog through *Stephen's Lighthouse,* and promise to start an SLA president's blog to keep everyone informed and start an interactive discussion with members—not just one-way communication, but ongoing conversations. A leader must have strong communication skills, and I think I can demonstrate that I bring this competency to SLA.

I believe in a leadership based on collaboration, teamwork, networking, and two-way communication. I can demonstrate that the teams I have led and participated in have been successful. I can also communicate the value of special librarians and information professionals to audiences other than us, as well as our vision for the knowledge-based economy. I have performance experience in the press, radio, and TV.

Focus, recognition, confidence, balance, learning, trust and respect, and calculated risk

We can reach a new plateau. We can prove our value to those we work with, work for, and get our funds from. We can achieve greatness. By the end of my term, I want more employers to know that librarians rock. I don't want anyone to say that they are having trouble finding a position as information professionals. I don't want anyone denying that there is a librarian shortage. I want employers fighting over the best and recruiting. I want employers that closed their libraries to fail (or become quite ill and cure themselves by hiring a librarian—grin). I want employers with great libraries to succeed and blame their librarians. That's how I want us to measure our success.

I hope that I haven't appeared arrogant—just confident that I can lead SLA. I am asking you to buy into this vision by voting for me. What's my great weakness? Impatience. Let's get on with it. Thank you.

Abram reminds us that we also must advocate
for and market ourselves, as individuals.

Marketing Your Valuable Experience

I am always amazed at the number of library marketing plans and marketing collateral that I have reviewed that market the library, the collections,
and the services, but do *not* talk about the *people* in the library. Rarely does
one see effective promotion of the "librarian," the catalyst for all of these
wonderful collections, networks, and services—and without whom they
wouldn't exist! Amazing, isn't it?

The reality is that people do *not* come to the library simply to access
information—otherwise we could truly set ourselves up as McInfonauts
and run a fast food operation, delivering infoburgers across a counter using
cheap high school labor. The reality of library services is this: the experience of acquiring the information is equally as important as the information itself. Effective delivery of information requires that it be digested as
knowledge by the ultimate user. This "transformation" of information into
usable knowledge is made possible through our professional skills, and
through our relationships.

The marketing activity of delivering effective information while
highlighting our personal qualities and professional attributes is key to
promoting ourselves. In a past life I jokingly referred to this as "vicious self-
promotion," but now I believe that it is a critical professional skill for our
survival and success. So I thought it would be useful to survey some of the
tools we have in our toolkits that we should be using to our advantage.

From *MLS: Marketing Library Services* 10, no. 7 (October–November 1996): 87–88.
Published first by Information Today, Inc. (http://www.infotoday.com). Reprinted
with permission. All rights reserved.

YOUR BIOGRAPHY

How many people out there have several versions of their biography ready for when they need them? You need more than your resume when you are marketing your services. Your resume is designed to get you a job; your "bio" is used to get you projects within your job. You need to have several bios in your virtual back pocket. You need to have a two-line bio suitable for the end of articles or for captions on pictures. You need to memorize a "sound bite" describing your contribution to your organization (which is distinctly different from your title and department) for use at corporate events, meeting introductions, and on the elevator when time is tight. And you need a bio that is a short paragraph that summarizes your education, experience, and talents for use in proposals, budget requests, project suggestions, or external communications.

YOUR SELECTED ASSIGNMENTS

You are not just the sum of your education and upbringing. Every project, reference question, report, and job you've had has added to your skills, talents, and abilities. A carefully selected list of these becomes an endorsement of your skills, highlighting important accomplishments. Don't just talk about the project and expect the reader to make the leap to *your* contribution. List each project by its name and sponsor, with a two- to three-line summary of the project and the results to which you contributed. Use this piece in your brochure, annual report, proposals, etc. Add to it over time, polishing your image—remember the old adage that history is written by the winners.

YOUR TALENTS, EDUCATION, EXPERIENCE

Do you highlight your talents and education in the vehicles available to you? Have you won awards? This can be promoted effectively and with class. If you or someone from your team graduates from a program of study or receives a professional award, hold a congratulatory party or reception. Highlight in your toast or recognition how this improves the team of people who deliver research. Ensure that your experience and expertise are well known. In many organizations, you are valued for your network, which is carefully built through the years!

YOUR "TEAM"

Make sure that all of the promotion of the "people" side of your marketing covers the whole team. Don't just cover the professional staff, but include everyone who contributes to the users' experience in your library. The library's image is the sum of these interactions, and is not driven only by getting the right answer to the right person at the right time.

YOUR PICTURE

Do you have a picture of yourself? Of your staff? What does it look like? Does it show you interacting with a computer? A book? Or an end user? Does it show you in the library or out in the organization? A picture truly is worth a thousand words—make sure that you choose the words carefully. Avoid head shots—a disembodied head floating in space does little to enhance your relationship with users or to communicate a story. A picture with people is worth more than one with equipment or collections—you want to highlight your contribution to the client's needs, not your relationship to your tools. A picture of two outside the library and in the mainstream will subtly but surely communicate your role in the greater enterprise. Remember to choose who you are pictured with carefully—it shows support for you.

YOUR PROFESSIONAL WORK

How do you communicate your memberships in your professional associations? Many librarians contribute to their professional associations like SLA, AALL, MLA, and the ALA. This can be impressive, especially if you can link it to your organization's needs. Highlight the network this creates for your organization, a network which would be lost if not for your own personal network. Do you volunteer on editorial boards for publications? I was amazed once when a lawyer I was talking to was unaware that the company librarian was on the editorial board for a major work of Canadian law. When I asked the librarian why she kept it so secret, she replied that she was worried that her employers might see it as not contributing directly to the firm's needs. But, in fact, the lawyer showed renewed respect for this librarian.

YOUR PUBLICATIONS

Do you write? And if not, why not? Seek opportunities to write not only for the library press but also for your industry or sector press. An easy way to start is to review books or to develop short lists of topical articles or websites for your industry's "rag." When you do, make sure you route it to interested users with your authorship noted on the covering memo. Post it on your bulletin boards. People will want to work with successful people if you position yourself as such.

YOUR FEEDBACK

Got thank-you letters or e-mails? Use them. Use these endorsements in brochures and articles. Make sure they highlight the person who delivered the service and not just a generic "library." Some people make the error of generalizing personal praise to the library—it's better to highlight the personal praise for professional service than to water it down. It's people who make the experience a positive one—not your collections, databases, or services.

MARKET YOURSELF—NOT THE COLLECTION

Avoid shyness and modesty! It's not in your professional or personal interest to hide your talents and abilities under a basket. It's also decidedly not in your organization's best interest not to make better use of one of their most important professionals.

In a capitalist economy, such as exists in most of the developed world, salary is one important—if not the most important—way that society tells individuals how much they are valued. Abram encourages strong advocacy of appropriate pay for librarians.

Pushing the Pay Envelope

Y2K Compensation Strategies

Are you happy with the perception of the value of special librarians in today's marketplace?

Why do so many librarians feel underpaid and undervalued? Where is the cash payoff in this, the knowledge-based economy? Of course, what we feel about this is not enough in today's business environment.

What are the specific perceptions decision makers have about special librarians that affect us directly in the paycheck? What do you need to know about pay and compensation systems to be fully armed? What specifically can you do to increase your compensation package—as individuals and as a profession?

In 1988, the SLA president Joe Ann Clifton set up an SLA Inter-Association Presidential Task Force on the Image of the Information Professional. Its purpose was to study whether librarians should be fighting a "buns and sensible shoes" image or attacking very specific erroneous perceptions about librarians in the minds of decision makers. Published in 1990, the data collected and analyzed by the Image Task Force showed us that our traditional approach to dealing with our perceived image problems had failed. I feel strongly that this is a key issue for our profession. Have we made any progress in the last decade? The answer is yes, we've made progress.

The task force discovered that, clearly, librarians should not be worrying about "buns and sensible shoes" cartoons or "Conan the Librarian."

First published in *Information Outlook* 3, no. 10 (October 1999): 18–24. © Special Libraries Association. All rights reserved. Reprinted with permission.

An avalanche of shocked and appalled letters to editors complaining about every perceived slight to special librarians serves only to position us as whiners. I believe that by acknowledging this sort of negative image, we reinforce the image in the way that saying "Don't think about green hippopotamuses" immediately makes you thing about green hippos. We must begin to accept that this type of superficial image problem is not our top priority issue. We need to deal directly with those issues and attitudes that have an impact on our pay packets.

LET'S GET OUR OWN HOUSE IN ORDER!

The results of the task force surveys of librarians (all segments of the profession were surveyed) showed that we had significant attitude issues in our own profession. Anecdotal information collected over the years since the survey suggests to me that we still have lots of work to do.

> Over 50 percent of librarians perceived that we (our profession and our colleagues) lack confidence.
>
> Only just over 30 percent of us "sought" promotion, especially at the lower pay levels. It's a truism that you don't get what you don't ask for.
>
> Over 80 percent thought the profession is task-oriented, in direct contradiction to our decision makers' perception of us as people/service-oriented. In reality, we're process-oriented, which, in our society, accrues higher pay levels and defines the usual image of a "professional."
>
> Sixty-eight percent thought our salaries were appropriate, which is sadly in line with the result that many of us think we're not highly enough regarded by our employers. Pay is the most tangible measure of the regard in which your employer holds you.

In addition, between 50 and 70 percent of librarians earning between $30,000 and $80,000 per year were satisfied with their perquisites and benefits. Since perquisites and benefits represent up to 25 percent additional remuneration on top of base pay, and with so many benefits calculated as a result of base pay and organization rank, this may be a detrimental position to take as an individual or for our profession.

It bears repeating that we must value ourselves before others will value us.

WHAT SPECIFICALLY CAN WE DO TO ADDRESS THESE PROBLEMS?

There are three areas that must be dealt with in our profession and through our professional associations that would seem to be a good strategy. First, on the individual level, we must each learn and understand the factors within our organizations that feed and support the salary administration system. These areas include job descriptions, job evaluation systems, job titling, and salary surveys. Second, on the political level, my personal belief is that we must demand laws that protect the rights of women and ensure compliance with pay and employment equity legislation. We must support moves toward strengthening these laws, narrowing the gender gap in salaries, and removing the "glass ceilings" which keep far too many professionals from achieving all of that which they are capable.

Outlined below are some basic things you can do to communicate your position more effectively.

JOB DESCRIPTIONS

Without a doubt, we need a lot of work in this area. We need job descriptions that accurately convey the nature, scope, and value of our jobs in terms that management will understand and reward. And since we often write our own position descriptions, it can be a self-inflicted wound. Just a few of the problems evident are as follows:

> We not only don't use enough action verbs, we often seem to go out of our way to avoid them. It is amazing how many information professionals feel the need to inventory the clerical aspects of their jobs.
>
> We don't just occasionally slip into library jargon, we positively wallow in it.
>
> Use management words and terminology. Find and use the terminology your organization uses to discuss results and success.
>
> Focus your job description on end results. Then focus these end results on your value to the organization's mission. Focusing on end results will force you to make the connection to the organization's ultimate needs and the role you play in achieving these. When you make this connection—make it explicit.
>
> Emphasize your contribution to the enterprise's primary mission.
>
> Prioritize those activities that deliver the most value, not necessarily those that take the most time.

Emphasize your human relations skills and how important they are to accomplishing the end results required of you. It is important to realize that most library jobs require influencing skills in the management of staff, dealing sensitively with users, reference interviewing, and negotiating contracts with suppliers.

Always include your professional activities. . . .

JOB TITLES

It is undeniable that your job title can set the tone of many, even most, of your internal organizational relationships, and often the perception of the community at large as to your value to society.

Many of the library titles in the corporate world seem to have been pulled from the academic or public library setting (head librarian; reference librarian; head, technical services; etc.). This is not the optimum strategy. Your job title should match your corporate or organizational culture in order to serve the strongest internal communication function. It may be more appropriate to use a title like "manager, library" in a corporate setting or "information research officer" in a banking environment.

However, the debate over a single, best title or the word *librarian* is distracting and truly counterproductive. The ultimate, important task of a job title is to communicate your role within your organization in the context of its unique culture and style. It matters not that your coworkers and peers call you "librarian." Most lawyers are called lawyers, and most doctors are called doctors and nurses are called nurses. They certainly don't let that stop them from being called partner, chief of surgery, or professor of obstetrical nursing.

Librarians often have difficulty separating our profession from our jobs. The job title "librarian" is insufficient to describe the breadth of opportunity opening up in today's world. . . . Librarianship can be practiced in a wide variety of roles and environments.

MARKETING COMMUNICATIONS

On our association level, we must now be prepared to build on our nascent public relations program in this area and design a program to target the group of people who influence our pay. We must be prepared to stress the true nature of our work, emphasizing the perception weaknesses from the surveys:

▌ Librarians are *proactive.*

▌ Librarians are adaptable and innovative.

- Librarians are strong, assertive individuals.

- Librarians are essential to twenty-first-century teams.

- Librarianship is a desirable career.

- Librarians are technological experts in our field.

- Librarians are content experts.

- Librarians manage large budgets and assets well.

Marketing special librarians and information professionals as key players in the knowledge economy and as catalysts for success in our enterprises is a critical long-term play that we must start now.

And last, on the personal communications side—despite all the tools, documents, and reports discussed above—nothing replaces a conversation and a personal relationship with your decision makers. Use the tools, like your position description, the SLA Salary Survey, or the title on your business cards, to initiate a conversation with your senior managers about your position, your role in the enterprise, and the future of your services. You have everything to gain from better understanding and everything to lose through organizational ignorance and an informed management.

Two

Technology
Everything from PDAs
to Google

*Technology needs to take a step back, like utilities, like heat
and light, and let the services and people come forward.*

We all use computers at work. In our efforts to create and manage computer systems, we can easily lose sight of the utility we're really striving to provide to other people. In this chapter's articles, Abram emphasizes that librarians must maintain a broad perspective of their own growth, and of the life paths of customers. Even when the technical tools and terminology seem to change really fast, *customer service* remains the constant aim. We can all adopt lifelong mindsets of learning to keep pace with the tools we need, the people we seek to assist, and, in turn, the particular tools that they prefer for their own learning and enjoyment.

It's All Good is a blog from three OCLC staff members "about all things present and future that impact libraries and library users." Abram often writes about communication technology—new gadgets and new systems—but always as it affects our customers or can help us interact with them. The following article is a characteristic reaction to Abram's ideas.

Stephen's Big Ideas

Alane Wilson

Stephen Abram is a one-man band—more energy than whole cheerleading squads and more good points than the biggest box of Crayola crayons. His latest article published at *SirsiDynix OneSource* is called "Five Big Questions to Drive Strategic Thinking."

His five questions are

1. Have our users changed in a material way? (Yes)
2. Can we relax a bit now that we've adapted to the last few *big* changes? (No)
3. Is there another big environmental or technological change on the way? (Yes)
4. Are we automating for the future? Or are we just automating nineteenth- and twentieth-century processes? (Sort of)
5. Do we have the energy, resources, flexibility, and the money? (Of course)

I read this article a couple of hours ago, and question 1 was a timely one for me because I'd been musing over the weekend on the stereotyping I think we are all guilty of, now and then, of "senior citizens" (a phrase I am not fond of). I hear from librarians frequently that "seniors" who use their libraries resist new technologies, and offer this as a reason not to change the status quo.

First published in *It's All Good,* November 14, 2005 (http://scanblog.blogspot.com/2005/11/stephens-big-ideas.html).

Well, my dad turned seventy this past June. I think he's probably pretty typical of his age and experience. He knows how to use computers because he's used them as adjuncts to his job in several different careers, and he's been using one for personal reasons for some time. He is web-savvy because he discovered the Web is a good way to find information and stuff (especially now that he lives in Panama). And he's also broken most of the records on his Xbox rally driving game. I gave him the Xbox and the game as a seventieth birthday present even though he'd never played any kind of video game. I picked the rally game because he used to be a rally driver, and he's driven several of the routes included in the game.

My point is that my dad learned about computers and the Web and video because these technologies all had a context for him: part of a job, a way to keep in touch, and as absorbing entertainment. He has a lifelong habit of learning, and it is this habit that defines people far more than their age. Older library users are not homogenous anymore than young library users are. But many library staff know very little about their communities of users beyond big broad clichés—a bad basis for designing services.

As Stephen says: "The general 'public' just ain't so general anymore," and I'll bet there are quite a few "senior citizens" in your library's community like my dad.

The Four Stages of Technology in Society

First-generation convergence. Technology stands alone; telephones communicate, televisions entertain, radios play music, computers process data, terminals process words, calculators do math.

Second-generation convergence. Broad-market tools go digital and move to the Web; your PC plays data, words, music, audio, and video and allows you to interact, communicate, and play.

Third-generation convergence. The tools get personal; your PCS phone lets you pick up e-mail, check stock quotes, get tickled by your calendar, and even talk! Your PDA lets you access your files and the Web and more.

Fourth-generation convergence. The tools move seamlessly into our lives (work and play); like the computers in your car, you just won't know they're there.

So, how should info pros react?

Brains. We *know* more than they do! We have *very* high information literacy skills.

Heart. We care about excellent customer service; we strive to meet their *real* needs.

Courage. We're out there every day doing this; we will survive and thrive.

Presented as part of Abram's PowerPoint presentation, "The Information Tornado: Toto, I Don't Think We're in Kansas Anymore!" (Alaska Library Association, March 10, 2005).

Channeling My Next-Gen Device

I am addicted to my Palm Treo. It's sad but true. I am hopelessly attached to my PDA. It's only a year old, but I'll miss it when I trade up. Sadly, I am the Post-it note of lovers, as I am already envious of its younger, newer, shinier sibling—with its clearer screen, swappable battery, and Bluetooth. Why is it that I can stay happily married to the same woman for over thirty years, yet want to trade up my gadgets every year—even though I, naively, in the first blush of romance, sign two-year contracts? Sigh.

SO WHAT DOES THIS HAVE TO DO WITH SPECIAL LIBRARIES?

The devices—BlackBerries, Palm Treos, HP iPAQs, fancy phones, etc.—are ubiquitous. Most of our key users in the special library world have some form of these devices. They are especially popular in auditing firms, the military, among consultants and executives, in medical enterprises, and among sales folks and investment and finance pros. Many of our colleagues use them too. The student population is among the highest-penetrated markets. If our users are getting addicted to these devices (and many are), and they are starting to use them in preference to laptops and desktops, what do our services look like? And that's just about those of us who serve adult users and fellow employees, where we still have time to catch up. Those who provide library services and information support to students

First published in *Information Outlook* 9, no. 3 (March 2005): 38. © Special Libraries Association. All rights reserved. Reprinted with permission.

have considerably less time, since their users have adopted these devices at an incredibly faster rate. Here are a few key questions to ask yourself.

1. DO YOU HAVE A PDA AND USE IT?

If you don't, you can't truly understand the environment of your users. This isn't one of those "I don't have to be a chicken to understand an egg" issues. This is experiential learning at its finest. Once you have experienced the features and functions, you can discuss it at a more informed level to address the usability issues. I am not saying that it's a perfect environment at all, any more than our carpal tunnel-inducing desktop environment is. But realistically, it's where the users are, and that's where we have to be.

2. HAVE YOU LOOKED AT WHAT YOUR E-MAILS AND ALERTS TO USERS LOOK LIKE ON A PDA?

This is important! Do your attachments work on their device, or will they have to wait to get to the office to see your brilliant search results or answer? If they need it *now,* then you're not meeting their needs. Can you coach them (or your IT folks) to provide the right applications for great information experiences? If you know that the e-mail will be read on a PDA, you should be knowingly crafting it for that environment—short, punchy, accurate, plain—just like you write in different styles for the Web, e-mail, print, or textbook.

3. HAVE YOU SEEN YOUR WEBSITES ON THEIR SCREEN?

If you deliver many of your services through a website or intranet, then you'd better check. Sometimes, actually more often than we would like, they just don't display well, or are too graphically intense to download quickly. This is what XML-based web design does really well. It can be designed to sense the device it is arriving at and modify its display sensitivities to display well—to actually be readable. That's pretty cool, and it doesn't require you to maintain multiple sites for different devices. As a side benefit, you also get a better foundation for ADA compliance.

4. HAVE YOU TESTED YOUR INTRANET'S USABILITY ON THE PDA TOO?

Can you or your users easily sign in? Are your firewalls blocking the domains of your users' telecommunications providers? Can you improve usability with some authentication procedure? After they get into the intranet, will users discover that the best information is locked in PDF format, for example, and they lack the PDA application to read it? Does information get delivered fast enough that frustration doesn't develop? A frustrated user is not in the right frame of mind to adopt new information, no matter how good, and apply it effectively to meet the business or enterprise need.

These are simple things to test. They're simple things to fix. What you don't know can hurt you.

PDA devices are no longer toys or gadgets for the innovator and early adopter populations. They are not status symbols for the rich or geeky. They are not just for teens and Millennials. These devices, in all their variety, are mainstream now, and users have a right to expect that our information and library services will work well in this environment.

Now, you do know how to IM or SMS through your PDA phone, right? Welcome to the thumbster world. You'll soon be keying thirty words a minute, with your thumbs serving a global population of users and being their personal information coach.

Social Software

Libraries are part of society (whose root word is something like *social*). Duh! So we should be very interested in anything that claims to be socially driven.

There seem to be a few social categories—blogs, instant messaging, Internet forums, Internet relay chat, massively multiplayer online games, media sharing (like photos, video, and MP3s), personals, social shopping, social bookmarking, social citations, social networks, and wikis. They all use the power of collaborating in large numbers to build community and knowledge. In terms of sheer power, it seems ready-made to serve the traditional library mandate as it evolves with technology and society. (Can you say Library 2.0?) Key questions:

1. What are they doing right?
2. What can we learn from them?
3. What can we copy?
4. What are the best features, functions, etc.?

I'm no expert, but the answers have to be somewhere in

▌ How they link people of like interests

▌ How they link people and content

▌ How the users define their own social networks and the purpose for them

First published in *Stephen's Lighthouse,* January 6, 2006 (http://stephenslighthouse.sirsi .com/archives/2006/01/social_software.html).

- How one might manage this so that it doesn't become "just dating"

- How they manage profiles

- How they manage "reputation"

- How they manage user-driven privacy level management

Are there some cool current library applications? I can imagine ones like this: book clubs, one-city one-book networks, homework circles, charitable clubs for foundations, local history clubs, genealogy clubs, antiquers, birders, old car buffs, mystery lovers, (auto)biography lovers, self-help, skateboarders or extreme sports fan clubs, gaming, philately, numismatics.

There are likely items in our collections to support most of these groups (sometimes users come in groups!). I actually like the idea of groups, since they help build community bonds and stave off loneliness for some. Either way, they connect to the human need to connect with information, entertainment, learning, and people.

It's interesting and sure provides the opportunity for us to extend our reach (and our collections' relevance) beyond the meeting rooms and the service desks. It also seems like it would be easy to pilot with a small targeted group, in order to learn cheaply and cheerfully. This is a bandwagon that sure provides a lovely sandbox for us (and for free on the Web).

Web 2.0—Huh?! Library 2.0, Librarian 2.0

Recently I was asked if some software applications I was involved in were Web 2.0-compliant. This was amusing and distressing on so many levels. It's amusing because what is being called Web 2.0 isn't a "standard" in almost any sense of the word. It's distressing because it shows how quickly a conversation becomes an expectation in today's world.

This is a perfect example of the power of the ninety-five theses of the Cluetrain Manifesto [http://www.cluetrain.com]. The major thesis is No. 1: "Markets are conversations." Anyway, I thought it might be useful to devote this month's column to a little information on Web 2.0 and its new-born babies, Library 2.0 and Librarian 2.0. And why should you read this column? You've heard it all before, but in a few years these Web 2.0 conversations will have the power to move huge transformations in your media landscape and therefore our life, work, and play environments. Sigh.

WEB 2.0

According to some sources, the term *Web 2.0* has been around since about October 2004. From *Wikipedia,* the free encyclopedia (gotta love the price), it is defined as "a term often applied to a perceived ongoing transition of the World Wide Web from a collection of websites to a full-fledged computing platform serving web applications to end users. Ultimately Web 2.0

First published in *Information Outlook* 9, no. 12 (December 2005): 44. © Special Libraries Association. All rights reserved. Reprinted with permission.

services are expected to replace desktop computing applications for many purposes" (http://en.wikipedia.org/wiki/Web_2.0).

I think Web 2.0 goes much further than this, actually beyond an application focus. It's really about the "hot" Web. I am talking here about "hot" in the McLuhanesque sense of the hot and cold or warm and cool aspects of technology.

What makes the Web warmer or hotter? Interactivity. Of course, the Web is already interactive in a cooler sense. You can click and get results. You can send e-mail and get responses. You can go to websites and surf. The old World Wide Web was based on the "Web 1.0" paradigm of websites, e-mail, search engines, and surfing.

Web 2.0 is about the more human aspects of interactivity. It's about conversations, interpersonal networking, personalization, and individualism. In the special library world, this has relevance not just to the public Web, but also to intranets and the imperative for greater social cohesiveness in virtual teams and global content engagement. Plain intranets and plain websites are fast becoming old stuff, just so last century. The emerging modern user needs the experience of the Web, and not just content, to learn and succeed. Context is the word of the day here. Such technologies as are listed below serve as the emerging foundation for Web 2.0:

- RSS (really simple syndication)
- Wikis
- New and revised programming methods like AJAX Mashups and APIs
- Blogs and blogging
- Commentary and comments functionality
- Personalization and "My Profile" features
- Podcasting and MP3 files
- Streaming media audio and video formats
- Reviews and user-driven ratings
- Personalized alerts
- Web services
- Instant messaging and virtual reference, including co-browsing
- Folksonomies, tagging, and tag clouds
- Photos (e.g., Flickr, Picasa)

- Social networking software

- Open access, open source, open content

- Socially driven content

- Social bookmarking

The technology infrastructure of Web 2.0 is complex, constantly in flux, and really in a Renaissance mode. It includes server software, content syndication, messaging protocols, standards-based browsers, and various client applications.

This is fundamentally about a transition of the website and e-mail-centric world from one that is mostly about information (and largely text information) to one where the content is combined with functionality and targeted applications. Web 2.0 can be seen as the Web becoming a computing platform for serving up web applications to end users, but I believe that this is a too geek-centric point of view. It's primarily about a much higher level of interactivity and deeper user experiences that are enabled by recent advances in web software combined with insights into the transformational aspects of the Internet.

Web 2.0 is ultimately about a social phenomenon—not just about networked social experiences, but about the distribution and creation of web content itself, "characterized by open communications, decentralization of authority, freedom to share and reuse, and the market as a conversation." To enable this new world, we will see a more organized Web with a plethora of new modalities or categorized content, more developed deep-lining web architecture, and a greater variety of web display modes, like visualization. Ultimately this will result in another shift in the economic value of the Web, potentially equaling that of the dot-com boom and probably driving an even higher level of social, political, institutional, and economic disruption.

What is truly exciting is that Web 2.0 is just the title of a conversation. There is no standard (at least not just a single one). We can all participate. To the detail-oriented, this conversation may be too high in the stratosphere with enough concrete recommendations, and to the theoretically inclined it may remain too visionary for real implementation. Among all of us, it is worth following. Web 2.0 is probably the series title of the most important conversation of our age, and one whose impacts will likely be truly transformational on a global scale.

WEB 3.0

There is even discussion and dreaming about a "Web 3.0." One could speculate that the Google/Sun Microsystems alliance to create a web-based operating system for applications like word processing and spreadsheets is an early indicator of this trend. Perhaps it's something like the Croquet Project, which is very exciting and worth reviewing [http://www.open croquet.org].* It is a potential scenario of what Web 3.0 might look like. Web 3.0 will probably be even more distributed in form than Web 2.0, and maybe some of the Web 2.0 applications will disappear or merge with a new integrated whole. Web services or the emerging semantic Web may replace such things as social networking sites and repositories.

LIBRARY 2.0

In the special library and information professional world, we generally deal with a savvier audience of users relative to the general consumer, and, indeed, a target that is easier to name and identify. This means that when our most critical users don't know about or use tools, we can inform them and train them in the newest technologies that can affect their success. For those users who can quickly become comfortable using technologies such as wikis, RSS, instant messaging, news aggregators, and blogs, we can help them to leverage these in making a difference in reaching their goals and their institutional or enterprise goals.

Library 2.0 is another "conversation." This narrative revolves around the concept of how to use the Web 2.0 opportunities in a library environment. It's an exciting concept, and one that can create a conversation that creates the next generation of library websites, databases, OPACs, intranets, and portals in a way that allows the end user to thrive and survive (and libraries along with them!).

Clearly every one of the technologies listed in Web 2.0 above—RSS, wikis, blogging, personalization, podcasting, streaming media, ratings,

---

* From the Croquet website: "Croquet is a combination of open-source computer software and network architecture that supports deep collaboration and resource sharing among large numbers of users. Such collaboration is carried out within the context of a large-scale distributed information system. The software and architecture define a framework for delivering a scalable, persistent, and extensible interface to network-delivered resources. Croquet is also a complete development and delivery platform. Its infinitely scalable architecture provides it with enormous possibilities as an operating system for both local and global informational resources." The project's Current Core Educational Partners are the University of Wisconsin, University of Minnesota, Massachusetts Institute of Technology, Kyoto University (Japan), University of Illinois Urbana-Champaign, University of Magdeburg (Germany), Columbia College, Boston University, San Diego State University, United States Military Academy at West Point, Cornell University, National Center for Supercomputing Applications. —Eds.

alerts, folksonomies, tagging, social networking software, and the rest—could be useful in an enterprise environment and could be driven or introduced by the library.

Yes, I know that many of these are used individually in many of your environments. The beauty of Web 2.0 and Library 2.0 is the level of integration and interoperability that is designed into the interface through your portal or intranet. That's where the real power to enhance the user experience is. To take advantage of the concepts inherent in Library 2.0, it is imperative to not shy away from adding advanced functionality and features directly into the content. This would provide the context and workflow-oriented features that users will demand or are demanding already.

Recently there has been a blog-based discussion about the need for renewed functionality in the ILS (integrated library system) and the OPAC. John Blyberg has promulgated an ILS Customer Bill of Rights* which asks for four things:

▌ Open, read-only, direct access to the database

▌ A full-blown, W3C standards-based API to all read-write functions

▌ The option to run the ILS on hardware of our choosing, on servers that we administer

▌ High security standards

While this list is largely focused on the systems librarian's needs list, it does provide a foundation for Library 2.0 for end users as long as we have Librarian 2.0 in place. Many of the requested aspects of Library 2.0 are already available in the ILS interfaces for those who choose to update to current versions. It just requires Librarian 2.0 to happen!

LIBRARIAN 2.0

Librarian 2.0 is the guru of the Information Age. Librarian 2.0 strives to

▌ Understand the power of the Web 2.0 opportunities.

▌ Learn the major tools of Web 2.0 and Library 2.0.

▌ Combine e-resources and print formats and be container- and format-agnostic.

---

* http://www.blyberg.net/2005/11/20/ils-customer-bill-of-rights/. —Eds.

- Be device-independent and use and deliver to everything from laptops to PDAs to iPods.

- Develop targeted federated search and adopt the OpenURL standard.

- Connect people and technology and information in context.

- Not shy away from nontraditional cataloging and classification and choose tagging, folksonomies, and user-driven content descriptions where appropriate.

- Embrace non-textual information and the power of pictures, moving images, sight, and sound.

- Understand the "long tail" and leverage the power of old and new content.

- See the potential in using content sources like the Open Content Alliance, Google Print, and Open WorldCat.

- Connect users up to expert discussions, conversations, and communities of practice and participate there as well.

- Use and develop advanced social networks to enterprise advantage.

- Connect with everyone using their communication mode of choice—telephone, Skype, IM, SMS, e-mail, virtual reference, etc.

- Encourage user-driven metadata and user-developed content and commentary.

- Understand the wisdom of crowds and the real roles and impacts of the blogosphere, web syndicasphere, and wikisphere.

First and foremost, Librarian 2.0 understands users at a deep level—not just as pointers and clickers. Librarian 2.0 understands end users deeply in terms of their goals and aspirations, workflows, social and content needs, and more. Librarian 2.0 is where the user is, when the user is there. This is an immersion environment that special librarians are eminently qualified to contribute to. SLA, with our Click University, should be well prepared to help our members to acquire and improve these skills and competencies.

It is essential that we start preparing to become Librarian 2.0 now. The Web 2.0 movement is laying the groundwork for exponential business growth and another major shift in the way our users live, work, and play. We have the ability, insight, and knowledge to influence the creation of this new dynamic—and guarantee the future of our profession. Librarian 2.0—now.

A Google Wi-Fi Network

Well, it's speculation time again. If Google did any or all of the following:

1. Provided free continent-wide broadband access?
2. Offered TV through this new network?
3. Offered movies or TV series like *Lost* or *The Sopranos* on demand through the network?
4. Delivered ads to cover some or all of the costs? (Remember when movies were free on TV and covered by ads?)
5. Offered VOIP telephone and integrated it with e-commerce? (Remember when we talked to people when we bought things?)
6. Provided an iTunes on steroids service that was compliant with the law(s) of commerce and ownership? I'm old enough to remember when my 45s cost 45 cents!
7. Expanded its alliance with Amazon and the A9 search engine to provide e-books and book access through Google Print as a finding tool?
8. And allied with Amazon and others to enhance Froogle?
9. And settled in for a strong local experience using their 3D maps of your town and defaulting to a local.google.com home page?

Soooooo—what would this do to local libraries of any type or stripe? What are the opportunities? Where will smart libraries position themselves in their communities?

First published in *Stephen's Lighthouse,* September 24, 2005 (http://stephenslighthouse
.sirsidynix.com/archives/2005/09/a_google_wifi_n.html).

Wireless Hotel Models

I end up using the wireless links in hotels a lot. Sometimes, rarely, it will work from your room. Usually it is free in the lobby, bar, and coffee shop. Maybe the profit on the coffee you purchase is higher than the hotel's share of the wireless link.

Hotels usually travel in packs. I've often left the hotel I am staying at to take advantage of the free lobby access next door. Tellingly, I'll frequent that other hotel the next time I visit. (I also find that when you phone to book your room, the staff have little idea of what kind of access they have.)

Despite these nightmares, I think there's much to learn for libraries from the hotel model. For example, when I use the hotel wireless, they somehow hijack my preferred home page settings and display local news, weather, and ads for other hotels in their chain. Hmmmm. How many libraries do this? Can we force a library home page as recompense for providing wireless access in our spaces? Can we promote our services by providing localized information like weather and sports? Can we be so bold as to promote events in other branches? Can we be so in their face as to blog library marketing?

At hotels there is also an access policy that you need to click through to use the free (or fee) wireless. I suspect more of us do this—always with the rules.

First published in *Stephen's Lighthouse,* September 20, 2005 (http://stephenslighthouse .sirsi.com/archives/2005/09/wireless_hotel.html).

Last week I heard a great story from a librarian who had to deal with reduced hours in her branches due to budget shortfalls. As she drove by a closed branch early one evening, she saw folks sitting on the front steps of the closed branch. Upon closer examination, she saw they were all working on their laptops. Weird—until she realized that the library's wireless access was on all the time and people were using the library from the stoop. Out came the digital camera for the photo op of a lifetime for her politicians and budgeteers! Libraries—filling local needs and delivering value. Maybe they need picnic tables out front under a wireless symbol. The Cleveland Public Library told me that the access in their sculpture garden was excellent, which seems like a cool place to surf, research, and study.

Competing with Google in a Special Library

I have been speaking a lot lately about how librarians must reposition themselves in a Google-manic world. Among end users there seems to be a lust and unchallenged adoration for Google searching. We know better (although, sadly, a few of our colleagues are throwing in the towel and recommending Google and linking to Google with unquestioning abandon!). Quality and targeted information comes from many sources and, yes, even sometimes from print. I have a ton of ideas and techniques for competing with Google. Here's a list of ten that seem relevant to special librarians.

1. START ELSEWHERE

When doing reference or research in front of a client, always use another search engine besides Google. If you are an information professional, what does it say to your client when you immediately click on Google and start searching? Does your client immediately think, "I could have done that!"? Do any of us seriously believe that our specialized searching skills and techniques are evident and visible to our clients? By starting with an unusual search engine like Exalead (http://www.exalead.com/search/), Grokker (http://www.grokker.com), Clusty (http://clusty.com), or hundreds of others, we show the breadth of our resources and skills and might even start a conversation about information literacy on the enterprise and intranet level.

First published in *Information Outlook* 9, no. 11 (November 2005): 46. © Special Libraries Association. All rights reserved. Reprinted with permission.

2. USE ANOTHER TOOLBAR

Do your users see you favoring the Google toolbar? It's handy, but shouldn't there be others in view on your browser? Do you have the various options for OCLC's Open WorldCat toolbar (http://www.oclc.org/worldcat/open/searchtools/default.htm) installed? Nearly every search engine has a toolbar now; download a few. Since search engine web crawls have so little overlap, good searching depends on using multiple search engines. Your users should see you recommending and modeling that behavior.

3. TALK RICHLY

Google doesn't talk to your users as well as you, although they will be pulling up to the side in the future. Their recent hiring of the developer of GAIM, an open-source multiple instant messaging protocol client, hints at a world where people communicate more richly in the Google world. Get better at IM, voice over Internet (VOIP telephone), Skype (http://www.skype.com), co-browsing clients like Jybe (http://www.jybe.com/site/index.aspx), and virtual reference services like Docutek (http://www.docutek.com). You can easily start with using multiple IM clients like Trillian (http://www.ceruleanstudios.com) and GAIM (http://gaim.sourceforge.net/downloads.php) and grow from there. It is as imperative to learn the ways in which communication will happen on the Internet as it was to adopt telephone and e-mail in the last century. (A few weeks ago, I read an old *Wilson Library Bulletin* article from 1957 arguing that libraries should not do telephone reference. What a hoot! There are certainly naysayers in every age!)

4. BE WHERE YOUR CUSTOMERS ARE

By this I mean have your presence available where your customers will trip over it. Whether you are dealing with an intranet-bounded client base or whether your group finds you through a public website, you must make sure your services pop to the top. If you offer services, tell them what they are. Indeed, a banner ad isn't necessarily evil. Can they find your phone number everywhere they have an information need? Can they find your IM handle, e-mail address, location, and snail mail address? You know how frustrated you get trying to find contact information hidden so slyly on the websites we use for research; why haven't we learned to solve that issue for ourselves?

5. KNOW YOUR USAGE AND IMPACT

This seems easy, but it's apparently hard. Of all the web pages and web content you contribute to, including your blogs, do you know how many times it's being used—hits, unique hits, unique users, and all the rest? Is it growing? What works to keep usage up? You must know what is working for your users. Spend time knowing your usage as well as Google knows theirs. Then act on your insights.

6. BE AWARE OF SEO

SEO means "search engine optimization." There is a community of search engine practitioners (including quite a few librarians) who hire themselves out to ensure that their clients' websites, products, and services show up on the first three pages of hits. In general, it can be the case that the hits you get on many search engines have been "optimized" or tampered with by persons for their own purposes. These can include corporate needs, special interest groups, or political needs. Start repositioning your services to deal with this major Google weakness in the library world of nonpartisan and unbiased results. Actually, we aren't unbiased; we are biased in favor of quality and balance. Do you choose content to select for your clients based on whether an advertiser has promoted it through payments to you (as is done for Google)? Do you allow your selection of content to be tweaked by special interest groups? Have you educated your users about this threat to the quality of their answers in Google and other search engines? Pew Internet and American Life surveys have shown that over 90 percent of users cannot distinguish between the ads and the results list on Google. I'll wager that 99 percent are unaware that the results can be tweaked by others. Shall we have a world where Google results are trusted over librarians?

7. BUILD COMPELLING CONTENT

What makes content compelling in your enterprise? I was talking to a past president of SLA, Donna Scheeder, whose team built a timely web page to support questions about the U.S. Supreme Court's nominations process and history. It quickly generated 85,000 hits. The trick was that they built it incrementally and responded to an expressed public need. This site [http://www.loc.gov/rr/law/nominations.html] now stands as an asset for the future that can be built upon. It also gets discovered in the top five hits on Google when you search "supreme court nominations." Compelling indeed! The lesson here is that we can increase our relevance by building compelling content. Compelling to my mind is timely, quality, rich, selective, deep, helpful, complete, and more. We know how to make content compelling. Let's keep getting it out there on the Web and on our intranets.

8. BE A "NEXTHEAD"

We tend to be "textheads" and promote the value of text-based content over or to the exclusion of other content. Competitive intelligence, for example, is not just about finding documents and newspaper articles. Are we using the podcast search engines? Are we searching the new programs that can be viewed on the Web? Are we covering the White House press briefings in real time instead of old transcripts? Are you or your organization worried about what's said about you there or on blogs? Blogs, podcasts, MP3s, and streaming media are part of our world—a big part; let's ensure we can deal with them as well as Google plans to. We have just enough time to do this on the personal relationship level we excel at in our organizations.

9. TARGET AND SPECIALIZE

For all of Google's wonders, it does not excel at answering the tough questions—the ones that begin with "how" or "why." It also surveys the basic public Web and not the content (which is a much larger corpus) in quality licensed databases. We would be wise to build targeted searches using federated search technologies on top of specially selected resources that meet the needs of the target searchers—medical, legal, biology, whatever. When we can delight the user by providing search-and-find experiences that match the users' real needs, they will choose our services for their important research needs.

10. TAKE A RISK

I've said this before, but the spoils go to those who take a chance. Information professionals are in a battle for the hearts and minds of our users. The Googles of the world are amazing transformational services, but they're not the be-all and end-all. The time for study is passing, and the time for action is here. We librarians must learn that when we study something to death, that death was not our original goal. Let's try to take action as often as we study the path ahead.

Technology is making it increasingly easy to provide good
distance-learning experiences for students and library
users. Abram has twenty suggestions for librarians in
using this technology. We have included only those of
Abram's suggestions that advance his theme.

Twenty Ways for All Librarians
to Be Successful with E-Learning

E-learning and distance education have been with us for a long time.
I even remember when my alma mater experimented with a television
campus. There have always been issues with distance, resources, and time
for learners to get the learning opportunities they need. Australian students
in the outback have been getting elementary and high school educations
for decades. PBS and NPR have supported education through television,
radio, and websites for a long time. However, they don't say that the Internet changes everything for nothing! Libraries and learning have been two
sides of the same coin since time immemorial.

Web-supported learning isn't just about school. But since libraries
traditionally exist largely in learning environments, we must ensure that
libraries and librarians are up to the challenge of demonstrating and proving their relevance in this changing world. Academic and college libraries
support curricula—faculties, programs, courses, and lessons—as well as
continuing education and research. Grade schools are blending web-based
learning experiences with classroom sessions. And from the core of the
special libraries world, corporate, law, and medical libraries especially are
being challenged by an ever-widening range of technical, managerial, and
global training offerings. Many e-learning systems offer access to articles,
e-books, databases, and other extended learning opportunities without reference to the roles of librarians. Libraries were relevant in the brick-and-

First published in *Information Outlook* 8, no. 12 (December 2004): 42. © Special
Libraries Association. All rights reserved. Reprinted with permission.

mortar campus paradigm—indeed, central to it—but how do we integrate their content and services into the virtual e-learning environment? E-learning is one of the fastest-growing segments of the web information space, and the majority of the top 500 companies are investing in it.

The big question is—can we be just as successful and needed when our students' and employees' learning needs are not near enough to our collections and staff? Is this an opportunity to move our services close to the learner's experience? In short—where does the ultimate virtual library meet virtual learning? Can we increase our impact on employee and student learning?

Following on the successful SLA seminar on e-learning opportunities for libraries that I presented in September 2004, here is a short brainstormed list of the "low-hanging fruit"—those tactics that libraries should investigate to achieve successful complementary services for e-learning and distance education.

Some definitions may assist here. IDC Canada defines e-learning as synchronous or asynchronous learning that is conducted over Internet, intranet, extranet, or other Internet-based technologies. An LMS is a learning management system where learners, instructors, and employers engage in learning strategies and processes. An LCMS is a learning content management system where the focus is on content development. It is used to create, store, assemble, and deliver personalized e-learning content in the form of learning objects. Learning objects are discrete learning events that are re-usable, re-combinable, and re-learnable.

OPPORTUNITIES FOR LIBRARIANS AND E-LEARNING

1. E-learning is a great opportunity to develop new partnerships. Learning tends to be at the core of most organizations' strategies—either explicitly like in educational organizations, or implicitly in for-profit areas where change management requires new learning and new processes. Permanent, respectful teaming with IT/IS, your faculty of education, pedagogists and curriculum experts, commercialization and product development, human resources, personnel and training, line managers, and anyone challenged by training and development needs within the enterprise.

3. Adding discovery mechanisms for learning objects is a no-brainer. If an organization owns or licenses e-learning courses, potential users should be able to discover them through the intranet, OPAC, or portals. It is clearly dangerous if e-learning becomes a content island within the enterprise.

6. The OPAC cannot be ignored. A well-stocked library makes the information and research assets of the enterprise discoverable. A link to the OPAC from within e-learning courses, distance education activities,

and learning portals and commons is essential. Ideally, this access should be contextual and integrated with other relevant resources.

7. We have built specialized access to specific resources like books, articles, and videos for many years—especially at the course level. If your integrated library system supports reserve room functionality and e-reserves, it is time to review where this is discovered. It can be linked from a course website, but we should consider providing access to relevant content at the point of need—the lesson level rather than just at the macro course or program level.

8. *Webliographies.* Although someone has trademarked this word, it still communicates best, for me, the concept of the web bibliography. Library subject experts have been designing these for decades, and these reading lists and pathfinders can now find new value and use by integrating them into the lessons and courses in e-learning support—including ensuring they have live links.

9. *Blogs and RSS.* These are recently popular technologies that libraries have adopted rapidly, and they are ideal to add a dynamic component to web-enabled learning. It's a great opportunity to feed the latest resources in context to a class or program. Recent news stories can provide learnable and teachable moments; the latest dissertations can feed doctoral seminars; and the latest news on IT and recent IT programming books can alert learners in technical courses to resources that inform their work and improve long-term corporate performance. Push content has developed a lot since it first arrived and is worth investigating again.

10. In the physical world, the learning enterprise—academic or corporate—can often be drawn as revolving around its library and intellectual and information assets. In the virtual world with online repositories, virtual libraries, and virtual classrooms, care must be taken to ensure that the full resources of the organization remain visible and available to all learners and employees. Library workers must seek opportunities to add "Ask a Librarian" buttons, instant messaging, and virtual reference and help services to every point of contact with e-learning registrants.

11. Content is not always free, and it can come with copyright and licensing restrictions. Libraries are well positioned with the e-learning content folks to partner on dealing with DRM, licensing, and rights clearances issues. Indeed, the library has often purchased rights to content that should not be repaid for. There are opportunities here for cost efficiencies.

13. Why refer to an article in a lesson and just leave it up to the student to jump through hoops to read it? The OpenURL standard can discover the legal copy of an article anywhere you have rights to it, or can drive the user to a document delivery service to acquire it. Many aggregators such as ProQuest offer features in their interface that allow you to create persistent

or durable links that can be accessed from anywhere authenticated users are viewing it.

14. Learners need good resources around information ethics. Many libraries have great web pages on creating footnotes and bibliographies. Many e-learning courses have an essay component. Why don't you add these learning objects to the lesson in each course where the essay or project is assigned?

15. We are rapidly entering a world where streaming media and audio servers will host huge collections for libraries. All of these should be discoverable and usable from within a class or lesson. Prepare for this eventuality. Much can be learned from access to medical videos, speeches, and images, for example.

18. Are your learners able to use these e-learning concepts? Some organizations have discovered that they needed to train their employees (and trainers) to learn or at least use, the full features of these systems. Companies such as Educational Testing Service (ETS) are offering information-literacy benchmark tests. There may be simply a training opportunity for libraries here to append to their other training offerings.

In the long run, the ideal learning approach will likely be blended—a combination of classroom face to face, one on one, reading, and virtual learning that is both synchronous and asynchronous. Tie that to an individual's learning style and you've got a powerful combination. Our challenge isn't to decide whether it's going to happen—it's to offer up a smorgasbord of great library innovation on the learning process by remembering that the root word of information is informing—the essence of teaching and learning.

Competing with Google

Google has accomplished a lot in a short time. Where does it fit in the world of libraries: how libraries can compete, complement, or cooperate? What are Google's strengths and weaknesses? What are ours? We need to understand things well enough to differentiate ourselves from our competitors and to invest and build upon those differences. The halo effect surrounding Google right now is palpable. We should question where its success comes from, and where it actually is a clear failure or suboptimal effort.

WHAT DOES GOOGLE DO WELL?

1. Google is first and foremost an advertising company. It has been so successful with its sponsored links that most searchers cannot tell the difference between an ad and a regular link.

2. Like most search engines, the rankings of the results, especially for links displayed on the first three pages, can be manipulated by SEO (search engine optimization) professionals. They serve their clients and can be motivated by a sincere desire to provide ads or links that are on point; or, more cynically, they can be partisan political, lobbyist, religious, or special interest groups of all stripes who desire to manipulate the information available to the searching consumer.

A version of this article appeared as "Waiting for Your Cat to Bark—Competing with Google and Its Ilk" in *SirsiDynix OneSource,* September 15, 2006 (http://www .imakenews.com/sirsi/e_article000645245.cfm).

3. Google excels at simple questions—ones that begin with who, what, where, or when. They downplay their poor results on the complicated questions of how and why.

4. Google does popularity ranking well, but is the popular answer always the best answer? Obviously not.

5. Google has been very successful in getting its various toolbars downloaded into browsers, allowing it to track user behaviors and grow its understanding of the eyes to which it seeks to deliver ads.

6. Google does beta products very well. They release completed products and call them beta and leave them in beta for a long time, often years. This deflects any real criticism because, after all, it's only beta!

7. Google's algorithms work well with text-based websites and objects like PDFs, spreadsheets, and PowerPoints, making them findable and retrievable.

8. Google Scholar and College Life (powered by Google) are moving into the mainstream of student life very fast as they build a product aimed at advertising to the younger generations who comprise the most desired sweet spot of advertising.

9. Google does maps pretty well. The recent integration of Google Local into Google Maps will allow Google to use this locally oriented space to attract ad market revenues where it currently under-performs, e.g., classified, yellow page, real estate, and local ads.

10. Last, Google does blogs well—maybe not as well as others, but for free the price is right.

WHAT DOES GOOGLE DO POORLY?

1. Google disguises its inadequacies in the area of how and why questions by the sheer volume of the other kinds of questions.

2. Google does IM poorly. If you're serving up links to web pages and ads, it is very difficult to also keep your mind focused on relationships and interpersonal conversations.

3. Google isn't even on the map in social networking, while MySpace and Facebook are attracting users. If Google acquires a major social site or pumps loads of cash into its Orkut social site which is doing well in Brazil, this could change.

4. Google is behind the curve on e-commerce. People trust Verisign and PayPal [which Google just bought].

5. Google still doesn't do non-text well. The growing importance of audiobooks, tunes, podcasts, streaming media, and video is too big a trend for anyone, including libraries and Google, to ignore.

6. Google does local (communities, neighborhoods, clubs, etc.) poorly. Libraries are pretty good at this space; can this be sustained? If Google sets its landing pages to default to a local page (for example, toronto.google.com) to dominate local advertising, will we be ready?

WHAT DO LIBRARIES DO WELL?

1. Libraries are nonpartisan, but we are not unbiased—we are biased toward our communities' needs, quality information and safe environments, user privacy, and protecting the record and empowering the user.

2. Libraries are all about community—workplaces, neighborhoods, research, and learning communities.

3. Libraries are about learning, schools, colleges, universities, and lifelong learning, and are not just about reading, literacy, and providing access to and delivering "content."

4. There is a difference between algorithmic ranking and filtering. Libraries filter; we select or provide the key tools for our users to select the best. In a world overwhelmed with information, this critical capability and talent trumps everything.

5. Librarians excel at improving the quality of the question before it is asked. Google tries to guess at the question and delivers a best-guess answer, which doesn't always work.

6. No computer is near ready to perform a search based on a well-done research interview. We need to promote and develop new respect for these skills.

7. Libraries excel at understanding context and delivering what is right for that context.

8. Whether we are the center of the campus, the school, or the community, libraries do local very well. Our challenge is to use the new technologies to extend our reach into the community—both physically and virtually.

9. Libraries do collections well. However, while we once bragged about collecting comprehensively, we now must move to collecting selectively to meet a need.

10. Our greatest strength is the personal human touch. Can we position this for the new age?

WHAT DO LIBRARIES DO POORLY?

1. We are poor at marketing and promoting the library and librarians. We lack confidence; we don't seek and sustain attention. I can't think of another institution that has consistently done such a poor job for so long. We need to develop some selling skills. Whether we like it or not, people pay, whether there's a monetary transaction or not. They pay for their library visit with time, taxes, prestige, and their own success. If we need more money, donors, bigger budgets, or whatever, it never happens without asking for the sale.

2. We fail to merchandise our offerings in a way that is engaging and culturally relevant. When our libraries are exceptionally well merchandised they stand out, but if we were all doing it right, the poorly merchandised libraries would stand out.

3. We must become better advocates for libraries. Since we must get more money, support, and donations, we must get better at influencing the folks who matter.

4. We like to think that libraries are good at collaborating—we aren't. We have more divisions and barriers than synergies.

5. We are known for books. This is both good and bad. We need to expand our positioning to more than books.

SO, WHERE IS THE LIBRARY OPPORTUNITY?

Librarians aren't just about search; we're about improving the quality of the question. If we focus on search, we are focusing on Google's best game. If we focus on the question and the human touch, the overall customer experience, then we will not only survive, we'll thrive. Here are ten key things that your library or you can do in a Google world to compete effectively and invent the future:

1. *Reposition the librarian.* Vastly more information is used outside the library than in libraries—and most of the access to that information is now virtual. The key contribution of librarians isn't collecting, organizing, and delivering the information; it's improving the quality of the question. We must place the library's programs and people at the center of the question space, spending more time on finding and understanding than searching.

2. *Know your market.* Our communities are changing. Society is more diverse by almost any measure, whether it is language, values, lifestyles, information skills, and more. We must become familiar with the huge new range of market and business analysis tools, derive insights from this information, and *act* on it.

3. *Rethink the repository.* We have created amazing vaults of content, but we must build repositories that meet our core missions and not just convert the "popular" or commercially valuable. We must make sure that we are not creating content islands. We must create a dynamic research space that aggregates and makes useful all the information in these vaults *and* brings them together with the rest of the world's information archives, commercial or not.

4. *Push content out.* Libraries need to get better at making people aware that something that might interest them is newly available, and do this by using alerting services, blogs, RSS feeds, and aggregators.

5. *Get on the bandwagon early.* I'd love to see libraries riding the crest of the e-learning wave; we have a big opportunity to create social spaces where information can be created, shared, and stored. Let's build an innovation sandbox and collaborate with each other to ensure the sustainability of libraries and our host organizations.

6. *Invent targeted search.* Users demand search-and-display options that match their needs, learning styles, and information literacy levels; display results must evolve beyond simple ranked lists. Libraries have the opportunity to offer *ad-free* results that are not influenced by anything other than the user's search criteria! We can offer users the ability to search just the content sets that match their needs and literacy levels: biology students can search just the science databases; sixth-grade students get the database results based on their reading level; and business searchers find results in their own product-specific area. Google is still focused on the broad consumer markets, not on the needs of researchers.

7. *Lead the wireless revolution.* Customers must have information when and where they need it, not just during our hours or at PC stations. Public libraries should become involved in citywide wireless projects; hospital libraries in PDA-based information services; and businesses in putting applications on their clients' BlackBerries. The library's community web page should be the default on our community wireless hot spots.

8. *Get into the community.* Are you aimed and positioned to place library resources and services on every local web page? Are the latest acquisitions of gardening books being fed through RSS to the

garden clubs' web pages? Are you present for teens on MySpace? Does your college have a Facebook presence? It will be hard to close a library that feeds information throughout the community.

9. *Make the library discoverable.* Does your library appear on the first page of results on Yahoo, MSN, and Google? If we want to survive, we must place our messages where the users are seeking answers and will trip over them, and today that usually means at Yahoo, MSN, and Google.

10. *Build content first.* It is basic to our profession that we understand deeply the communities we serve. We serve many communities in many sectors and work alongside them, not as machines and algorithms to service them. We need to empathize with users' goals, psychological needs, and competency levels.

A CHANGING CLIMATE

Librarians are well positioned to thrive. But the future is not what it used to be. Our enterprise is no longer an extension of the past; everything is constantly changing, quickly. We have evolved many times over the long and great history of libraries. We can do it again.

Intelligent Conferences

Reality or Oxymoron?

Stephen Abram, with Rebecca Jones

Technology is having an impact on all areas of our lives, but until recently, it only seemed evident at conferences in lavish graphic presentations. Now it has begun to shake these five pillars, nudging each to test for stability. Just what impact will technologies have on all those conferences and educational events we so enjoy attending? Will we, in fact, attend them electronically or virtually? Will a log-on ID and password replace an airline ticket? Are the days coming to a close of trying to cram as many sessions as possible into our itinerary, while still leaving time for a strategic shopping strike and, of course, networking in the bar or nearest restaurant?

THE TECHNOLOGY OPPORTUNITY

Three trends have begun converging to impact our future conference experiences:

1. Attendee expectations are rising as loyalty decreases. Today's conference attendees want a more intense learning experience—probably more than can be delivered in the confines of a time- and site-limited event. When that rise in expectation combines with the individual's essential, personal professional development strategy of continuous learning, an annual stand-alone event just won't cut it.

From *Searcher* 9, no. 1 (January 2001): 42–48. Published first by Information Today, Inc. (http://www.infotoday.com).

Professionals need to continually upgrade their skills and acquire new ones. Opportunities for professional growth need to be continual, year-round, rather than once or twice a year.

2. The convergence of the technologies needed for communications, networking, and sharing knowledge and learning has reached the desktop. Bandwidth issues of the past are lessening, and the trend toward effective, on-demand e-learning experiences is burgeoning.

3. A more competitive environment for learning opportunities has arisen, with hundreds of new entrants starting to market new technology-based learning products, and with older players, like universities, getting into the distance-education space and competing for seats, eyeballs, time, and dollars.

The need to continuously learn, network, and grow is paramount to high-performing information professionals today. They face a challenge in locating and attending suitable opportunities, deriving value while there, and, finally, assimilating and building on the learning and contacts made after the event, when they're back at work applying their acquired knowledge and seeking out the next opportunity.

Conference providers can implement changes in two ways. First, *improve the core conference experience* to enable delegates to derive maximum benefit while there. Second, take advantage of the recently introduced technologies to *offer pre- and post-conference value* for delegates.

STEPS WAITING TO BE CLIMBED

So, how do conference planners provide richly textured pre- and post-conference learning and networking opportunities, allowing delegates to discuss what they have learned, follow through with speakers, share presentations with colleagues back at the office, etc.? Delegates want to see concurrent sessions they missed, contact like-minded learners, develop learning networks, and extend their learning experience with advice from pros, demos from exhibitors, and chances for brainstorming and debate. Conference planners and exhibitors also want to build their relationships with attendees, probing them about their evolving needs, expectation levels, and future plans.

What technology can help them do this? How can conference planners extend the conference experience and enhance their attendees' learning? The trick lies in the early adoption of such new technologies as web broadcasting, web collaboration software, profiling software, communities of interest, and distance-education software.

The biggest opportunity comes from integrated collaboration and conferencing environments. These have a suite of features that fit the conference and learning experience like a glove, just waiting for savvy and visionary conference planners to experiment with them. Here is a list of what some of the features will include: shared web browsing, PowerPoint presentations, application sharing, content sharing, streaming audio/video, shared whiteboard collaboration, polling and transcript capabilities, multiple presenter support, dynamic session control and remote participation, one-to-one and one-to-many or many-to-many comprehensive question-management functionality, and storing templates.

ENHANCING THE EXPERIENCE

How do you apply technology and thoughtful planning, marketing, and communication to enhance your market's learning experience? In the short term, we'll go out on a limb that for starters you need to investigate and experiment within these areas.

> Electronic registration will offer a wealth of opportunities to customize the experience to niche learners' needs, communicate effectively and in a highly targeted way with registrants, and allow the attendees to personalize their experience through the creation of on-demand networking experiences. Attendees share their profiles and e-mail addresses in return for a commitment to provide a personalized, customized, valuable learning experience.

> First-timers to regular conferences should be mentored and advised virtually and/or with an F2F (face-to-face) buddy at the conference in order to get the most out of their conference investment. Effective attendee profiling and communication systems would ease the overhead of managing this sort of process.

> Designated major programs, such as continuing education workshops and technical presentations, will have a pre-work and follow-through in a web-based collaboration environment. This should be more than reading lists! You should have the opportunity to play with the websites, intranets, and software that the speaker discusses.

> Keynote presenters will broadcast to larger audiences than just those bums in seats at the event. Keynoters will plan for online, web-based debate and stay to clarify their remarks for a determined time after the presentation.

Digitally recorded sessions, along with their graphic presentation materials, will be available for lease, license, or purchase on or through the conference organizer's website. Conference tapes will become a thing of the past, replaced by MP3 or some other digital sound file downloaded wirelessly to your car player. This could become a Napster for learning!

There will be more learning modes and models out there in the coming decade, rather than less. Competition is intensifying for people's attention, time, and dollars. We will see mergers and alliances between many of these new e-learning modes and organizations.

E-Learning Basics for Librarians

Why is e-learning important?

> People need to learn—and take action quickly.
> People are rarely in the same place where the learning is needed.
> Work still needs to be done! Productivity can't be reduced.
> Stuff will need to be invented, processes changed.
> Innovations will need to occur.

Desired benefits of corporate e-learning:

> Improved speed and effectiveness of the training process
> Ensured compliance with relevant industry education standards
> Heightened efficiency of supply chains through better product/ service knowledge
> Improved communication among and retention of employees during the business transformation process

Learning content management systems (LCMS): focus is on content development.

Learning management systems (LMS): focus is on training administration.

Excerpted from "E-Learning Basics for Librarians," a virtual conference delivered by Abram for the Special Libraries Association, September 29, 2004.

Criteria for selecting e-learning solutions:

> Understand the business issues that are driving the requirement for an e-learning solution and understand your culture
>
> Performance management processes
>
> Culture
>
> Resources
>
> What the technology needs to do
>
> Select the technology type that best addresses the issues: ease of use, ease of integration with other business applications, compliance with standards, scalability, customization, ability to incorporate array of media types, internal and external support. As always, consider the vendor.

The role for libraries in e-learning:

> Developing new partnerships: IT/IS, HR, personnel, and training
>
> Adding discovery mechanisms for learning objects
>
> Archiving learning objects
>
> Plug-ins from library [connecting e-learning to library resources such as] OPAC, e-reserves, webliographies
>
> Also handling DRM and rights clearances, database access and federated search, OpenURL and persistent or durable links, contextual footnotes, footnote and bibliography learning objects, streaming media and audio servers and collections, coursepacks and e-coursepacks, collection development services, information literacy training and testing, authentication, push content via RSS and alerts

Playing and Learning

Making a Sandbox for Librarians

I've been asked a load of times how library workers can learn all these newish technologies. I don't know why it's easy for me and difficult for others. I do a few things:

> I play.
>
> I surf sites, blogs, and articles that friends recommend.
>
> I schedule it.
>
> I don't stay committed if it isn't fun or engaging.
>
> I don't feel the need to learn every feature and nook and cranny of the site.
>
> I share. I don't feel guilty if it isn't directly applicable today to my current needs.

First published in *Stephen's Lighthouse,* February 22, 2006 (http://stephenslighthouse
.sirsi.com/archives/2006/02/playing_and_lea.html).

Three

Communities and Generations

The Library's Clientele and How It Is Changing, and the Differences between the Generations, Focusing on the Millennials

The next step in libraries is what are we going to do to "trick" our new users to use the library?

Technological divide: Everyone under twenty-five has an IM account, but most librarians over thirty don't. This needs to change.

This chapter includes some of Abram's most important work. In these writings he discusses the attributes of the current and the next generations of librarians and library users and points out how libraries and librarians must change in order to keep the Millennials as library users and to integrate them into library staffs.

Communities

From the User's Context In

I thought I'd start this column off with one that covers one of the underpinnings of my philosophy and my library and information strategy: how to view new technologies and how to choose great ideas and tactics.

Simply put, I think all great enterprises are built from the user in, not from the content out. Nor are great enterprises based on the available technologies and resources. Of course, that doesn't mean that some folks don't try and build success on a foundation of technology. They just aren't "great" in my opinion.

In order to build your enterprise strategy from the outside in, you have to know—and understand deeply—your user *in context*. That context is their individual role and place in the community. We know who our users are. Whether we call them users, clients, customers, learners, students, colleagues, or whatever, *what* is community—and how many types of communities are there? Is community like good art; we'll know it when we see it?

Libraries have long served many communities in many sectors. This is our *context*. We may exist on the premise that we improve the quality of questions, organize the world's recorded knowledge, preserve culture, and deliver the right content experiences for our users, but overall, we live in the context of our users. When we define that context as a "library" we miss the opportunity to truly connect with our users and their communities.

First published in *SirsiDynix OneSource,* January 2005 (http://www.imakenews.com /sirsi/e_article000342351.cfm).

It behooves us to understand, and understand deeply, the communities we serve. We need to empathize with their goals, their psychological needs, and their competency levels in each of the variety of communities that we serve. My colleagues and I at SirsiDynix spend a great deal of time thinking about this. We need to understand how our products, services, and software are being used and in what context. We need to focus on the true needs of the end user as well as the context of the service professional, the library worker. This has led us to think deeply about "context" and how many contexts there may be.

We, and our clients, also look at the opportunities provided by the variety of old and new technologies that relate to or enhance community development and interactions. These technologies surely extend beyond this list:

- Discussion lists
- Virtual classrooms
- Virtual reference
- Bulletin boards
- Kiosks
- Wireless
- Expertise database and KM tools
- Next-generation devices
- Communities of practice
- Social networking software
- IM buddy and e-mail nickname lists
- Productivity solutions
- Intranets
- Workflow enhancements

All of these can comprise the technological components of context management solutions. However, in order to plan strategically for technological and other process innovations, I believe that there must be a simple taxonomy of communities that can help us, as library leaders, to develop a framework for strategies and plans to serve our organizations and society—in context. Modestly, I propose the theory that there are only *five* types of communities that really matter to libraries. I have cogitated on this for a while, and here are the simple "five" communities:

1. Neighborhoods
2. Workplaces
3. Entertainment/culture
4. Learning
5. Research

These five apply at the level of each human user, as well as to the many information-hungry sectors: academic, college, public library, not-for-profit or for-profit enterprises, associations, and so many more. Obviously, each library user, or potential user, doesn't fit neatly into just a single community. Everyone, including ourselves, shifts fluidly between these communities—doing research, doing our jobs, and sometimes finding enjoyment in each—and learning a little along the way while living in our neighborhoods with our friends and families. The difference is that *in certain contexts* one community rises to predominant strategic importance and, therefore, takes planning precedence.

Let's quickly review each community.

NEIGHBORHOODS

At first glance, this feels like the public library niche. However, you can belong to neighborhoods in today's world that are not traditional. Neighborhoods can be bounded by their interests—not necessarily geography. They can be local, regional, or global—or even unbounded. *Communities of interest* are neighborhoods of people of like mind and focus. Sometimes those interests can be expressed locally and also find their niche on a broader scale. Think of the genealogical research revolution, knitters and needlepointers sharing patterns, or even Trekkies and Trekkers. People build neighbors through their interactions with their local institutions and religious experiences. People find their own comfort levels with their neighborhoods, and libraries can facilitate this by adding to their networks of neighbors and information providers to empower these communities with information and provide a sense of place. Libraries can provide decent and coordinated access to the resources of the whole community and not just the library. Libraries can provide context for their community to thrive.

WORKPLACES

Simply getting the job done creates communities. We create organizations because most work is too complex or complicated to be done alone. We can connect through contiguous offices and communication devices like telephone and e-mail. We connect in meetings small enough to surround the water cooler or big enough to use meeting rooms or auditoriums. Recently, we have extended these workplace communities through conferencing software, virtual reference, e-mail, and instant messaging. Intranets for most workplaces can also provide environments for workplace sharing. We see a trend to expanding these through the addition of interactivity and collaboration tools. Last, there are new professionally oriented communities that have moved beyond annual conferences and scholarly publications and have developed professional *communities of practice*. Libraries can play a key role in these communities when we align our magic with their ecologies.

ENTERTAINMENT/CULTURE

Most libraries serve some entertainment or cultural function. Many people find their jobs and positions engaging. Public libraries have long served a community's entertainment needs with recreational reading collections, nonfiction collections such as those aimed at celebrity fans, music aficionados, hobbyists, some genealogists, and all those gardeners and cooks. Many things that we define as entertainment are also indicators of our culture—music, plays, fiction, television, theater, celebrity, performance, etc. When we look critically at the Web, we can see a plethora of fan and hobby sites serving the need for entertainment and, indeed, preserving and animating cultural activities. An enriched OPAC plays a wonderful role in serving this function.

LEARNING

People come together in communities to learn and teach together. We identify these as classes, schools, courses, degrees, programs, certificates, and other forms of continuous learning. Libraries are struggling with how to provide information and research support for the emerging blended-learning environments. Learning is no longer restricted primarily to in-person classrooms and training seminars, but now comprises an amazing range of e-learning options. Our library-oriented initiatives now focus on the creation of learning commons and information commons to provide both physical and virtual learning spaces. As we plan strategically for the future, we must focus on ensuring the relevance of libraries in a world where learners expect learning and learning support at any place geographically, synchronously, and asynchronously. This will challenge all libraries deeply in the coming decade.

RESEARCH

Research communities fall into three main groups: personal, commercial, and academic. Few libraries are purely research, and few libraries don't have a research component to their services. It's a mistake to not explicitly recognize research as a key community in its own right. Researchers will generally self-identify their attachment to their community—historians, medical researchers, scientists, and others. Basically, if you believe you're in a community and others agree, then, de facto, you are. What has changed in recent years has been the ease with which research communities have found those of like mind. It is amazing to view the explosion of new research communities as people find others who know things they want to share and want to read and view the research results and opinions of others. Libraries have long served the research community. What has changed is the emerging trend to interdisciplinary research and the speed at which some disciplines are discovering new things without benefit of the scholarly publishing process (for example, cloning, DNA studies, robotics, bionics, human genome work, etc.). It's exciting, but it does present challenges for our profession with our focus on traditional recorded knowledge.

CONCLUSION

It's no mistake that these five groups of communities have three things at their core:

1. They all have a connection between people *first*. No amount of technology, communication, and fiat can create a community from whole cloth. Some human relationships need to exist first.

2. They can all be improved and empowered with the intelligent application of technological solutions that are aligned with the users' profiles, rather than expecting users to align their skills with the technology.

3. A new model of community development is emerging, with its own challenges, and all the while, the traditional models will continue to be useful and relevant.

The community—our customers—is not a homogeneous block. Abram points out that there are many ways to describe and evaluate a community.

Mars and Venus and the Internet

One of the new Pew Internet and American Life reports is called "How Women and Men Use the Internet." It notes that women are catching up to men in most measures of online life. It observes that men like the Internet for the experiences it offers, while women like it for the human connections it promotes.

> The percentage of women using the Internet still lags slightly behind the percentage of men. Women under thirty and black women outpace their male peers. However, older women trail dramatically behind older men.
>
> Men are slightly more intense Internet users than women. Men log on more often, spend more time online, and are more likely to be broadband users.
>
> In most categories of Internet activity, more men than women are participants, but women are catching up.
>
> Either way, with our primary use mode migrating to web-based users, we would be wise to know if this population of users is different than our "traditional" mind-set of users. Of course, we would then need to make sure we're building the right environment for them, testing it with the right folks and displaying the right content.

First published in *Stephen's Lighthouse,* January 1, 2006 (http://stephenslighthouse.sirsi .com/archives/2006/01/mars_and_venus_1.html).

Understanding Adoption Types

Innovators:

> Technology fascination
>
> Motivation—implement new ideas
>
> Confidence level high—experiment, risk
>
> Self-taught, independent
>
> Latest technology, few features, performance
>
> Self-sold, when turned on, word of mouth

Early adopters:

> The coming thing
>
> Motivation—leapfrog the competition, prove business
>
> Willing to try new things, reasonable risk
>
> Will attend night school to learn
>
> Innovation, better way to do job, selective
>
> Sold on benefits, references, word of mouth

Excerpted from Abram's PowerPoint presentation, "Working with Decision-Makers: Being a Trusted Advisor in a Time of Rapid Change" (Canadian Association of Special Libraries and Information Services, Toronto, Ontario, November 1, 2004).

Late adopters:

> Obvious solutions to problems
>
> Motivation—social pressure, fear of obsolescence
>
> No risk, slow to change, needs references
>
> Seminars, proven products, hand holding
>
> Brand important, pay for needed features only, terms and conditions important
>
> Examples, address cost/technical support

Laggards:

> Absolute need
>
> Extreme competition/social pressure
>
> Reluctant to change
>
> Will send someone to a seminar, needs proof, ease of use
>
> Lowest cost, competitive terms, brand
>
> Productivity increases, fear

Virtual Reference

I like to consider the big picture—the really big picture. These technologies are not just about serving up our reference services virtually. They're about putting the librarian back into the virtual space! Think about it. We are rapidly moving to the time (if some libraries are not already there) where the vast majority of our interactions with our users will be virtual—website hits, patron-driven ILL, remote database searching, and on and on. Loads of this happen with very little (or no) interaction with the humans in the library—librarians, information professionals, and library workers—that improve the service. While our virtual services deliver information quickly, they don't improve the quality of the question which has been reference librarians' stock-in-trade for more than a century. If we want to improve, and remain and stay relevant, we have to discover the virtual reference modalities that work. That requires a lot of experimentation, sharing, and cooperation. It's an exciting field right now as technology moves into the user space more and more.

First published in *Stephen's Lighthouse,* July 12, 2005 (http://stephenslighthouse.sirsi .com/archives/2005/07/virtual_referen.html).

In this article, written while he was president of
the Canadian Library Association, Abram continues
with his "big picture" analogy. It is best read by
mentally replacing "Canada" with "society."

Influence

It Takes a Fine Hand

Real movements influence society on a grand scale—and the library movement is no different.

Other movements focus on moving society in positive ways—the environmental movement, the women's movement, the civil rights movement—
trying to make society permanently better. We do too. We're part of the
new millennium's information economy and the knowledge-based society.

WHAT DO WE CARE ABOUT?

What do libraries, library workers, and information professionals really
care about? We care about the big picture:

1. Preserving Canadian culture
2. Preparing Canada for the global knowledge economy
3. Educating for the future: Addressing the competency gap
4. Ensuring equity for Canadians
5. Ensuring an innovative nation: R&D
6. Strengthening Canada's communities
7. Ensuring the benefits of e-government
8. Focusing on children
9. An investment in libraries is an investment in our nation's future

First published in *Feliciter* 50, no. 5 (2004): 172–73.

INFORMATION PROFESSIONALS AS SUBVERSIVES

One of the things I love most about our profession is that we are so subtly subversive. We create quality collections to parallel the morass of the Internet. We challenge ignorance. We encourage all children to read—even if some parents neglect this aspect of their foundation for success. We quietly but actively seek to free up the flow for *all* information and cultural and artistic works. We stand for user rights and balance in information access and copyright. And, as the T-shirt says, "There's something in my library to offend everyone!" And that's wonderful.

In his presentation, "Understanding End Users at a Deeper Level: Personals, Usability, and Norms," delivered to the American Library Association at a 2004 meeting in Chicago, Abram laid out a very similar list of library/librarian concerns. We've mapped them to the list in the preceding article, "Influence."

What Are Libraries Most Worried About?

1. Sustaining relevance (nos. 1 and 3)
2. Millennial user behaviors (3 and 8)
3. Diversity services, broadly defined (4)
4. E-learning and distance (2)
5. Justifying growth and projects—measures, not stats (5)
6. Understanding mutating (not changing) usage patterns—information, not data, *virtual* use (7)
7. Building community alliances, but bringing gravitas to the table (6)
8. Building for the future and not repairing the present (9)
9. Productivity and shifting staff resources (none)
10. Balancing print, electronic, and new services and resources (7)
11. Budgets and fund-raising (none)

Abram has in-house examples of Millennials.
He wrote this description of his children
especially for this book.

My Millennials

I have two kids, Millennials,* from whom I learn a lot. I call them my little laboratory rats—and only half in jest. To this I add the perspectives that I learn from my wife, Stephanie, who has taught every grade from five through thirteen as well as written many successful textbooks, websites, database guides, and teacher guides for many subjects and grades.

As of mid-2006, Zachary, my son, is twenty-one and Sydney, my daughter, is eighteen. Both are, in my opinion, highly representative of their cohort. You might recall these names as the characters Sydney Claire and Zachary Jared in the story in the first chapter.

Zachary surprised me in grade ten by producing an animated slide show called "Digital Dad" which consisted of a series of pictures of myself set to the tune of "Cat's in the Cradle." This was a none-too-subtle hint that I was spending too much time on the road and could be replaced. However, I did see the beginning of a generation that was developing a facility with multimedia communication. They'd gone beyond simple notes or oral complaints.

By grade twelve, Zac and a team of his cohorts were producing their culminating history project for graduation. They had to use primary

---

* For more on this generation, see the Beloit College Mindset List (http://www.beloit .edu/~pubaff/releases/mindset_2009.htm). The list for the class of 2009 includes: "2. They don't remember when 'cut and paste' involved scissors. . . . 16. Voice mail has always been available. . . . 49. Libraries have always been the best centers for computer technology and access to good software. . . . 61. Digital cameras have always existed." There is a similar list for New Zealand at http://mindset.massey .ac.nz. —JAS (Beloit class of 1969)

sources and develop an editorial opinion on a current event. The Iraq war had just begun (I flew on the last plane out of DC before the war started) and provided the perfect current event to document. When their plan to visit the Canadian ambassador in DC fell through due to travel restrictions, the team chose to visit Ottawa and videotape the opinions and perspectives of embassy staff, university professors, members of parliament, and others. They also taped their editorial opinions in front of appropriate places like the Canadian War Memorial, the Canadian Peace Monument, and the Canadian War Museum. In the end, they had eight hours of video that they distilled to a one-hour television program, complete with commercials and person-on-the-street interviews. This was accomplished by normal students, in a public school in inner-city Toronto. Each student managed to develop a thesis and communicate his or her point of view very effectively. This is a definite shift in ability and aptitude. Indeed, the crew stayed together and created a poignant end-of-school video documenting their years together at high school. None felt that this activity was anything unusual for their cohort. Zachary went on to publish a quarterly paper zine in university which included an e-mail feedback loop. "Paper is just edgier," is my favorite quote from my son.

Sydney, on the other hand, has talents that lie in a quite different direction. Her learning style is far more experiential, physical, and artistic. I learned from my daughter that reading, writing, and arithmetic are not the be-all and end-all when determining an individual's strengths and talents. Sydney does fine with the traditional three "Rs"; however, from an early age it was clear that her social skills, artistic ability, and physical skills were her real gifts. Sydney forced me to learn and acknowledge the roles our learning styles play in our adaptation of information and learning. Sydney has become an award-winning gymnast and has coached university gymnastics programs since she was fourteen. She has also learned to dance and do choreography and wins awards there too. Her talents are also evident in her musical abilities for vocal, rhythm, and viola as well as her work with performance art. Her physical, experiential learning style also shows in her artistic ability and the portfolio she has used to be accepted into fashion, fine art, and multimedia university and postsecondary programs. Her digital documentaries are interesting portals into the mind and opinions of this generation. She shows her high social skills in the huge number of instant messaging buddies she maintains contact with and that she has collected for years.

Both kids now maintain Facebook sites and continue to teach me interesting things about the nature of this coming generation. We all have access to this pool of talent and need only keep our minds open.

Dealing with the Generations
New (and Free) Must-Read Studies

Generational change happens almost imperceptibly, but it does happen; it comes up behind you and bites you in the ego. Several major studies were released at the end of 2002 that allow us to read the tea leaves of what exactly might be coming up from behind.

Are they—Gen X, Y, and Z—really different?

- Were the Boomers different for having been the first generation to grow up with TV?

- Were the Boomers' parents different for having grown up during a world war?

- Were the Boomers' grandparents different for having grown up in a depression?

Are they—Gen X, Y, and Z—really different? Of course they are!

- Gen X is the first generation to have had personal computing for their entire lives.

- Gen Y is the first generation to have the World Wide Web for every high school year.

- Gen Z is the first generation that will live wirelessly on the Web for most of their lives.

First published in *Information Outlook* 7, no. 1 (January 2003): 46. © Special Libraries Association. All rights reserved. Reprinted with permission.

We will be, or already are, meeting these people in our work. They've been in the schools and colleges for years. We had better understand how their information-seeking skills, research preferences, and analytical behaviors differ from those of previous generations. The following studies will give you some insights into what's on the horizon.

The OCLC's "White Paper on the Information Habits of College Students" [http://www5.oclc.org/downloads/community/informationhabits .pdf] is an excellent, free study that provides data on students' preferences in dealing with library and research information. It concludes with some tough questions for libraries and library staff to ponder strategically.

"The Digital Disconnect: The Widening Gap between Internet-Savvy Students and Their Schools" [August 14, 2002; http://www.pewinternet .org/report_display.asp?r=67] and "The Internet Goes to College: How Students Are Living in the Future with Today's Technology" [September 15, 2002; http://www.pewinternet.org/report_display.asp?r=71] are both from the Pew Internet and American Life Project.

"Dimensions and Use of the Scholarly Information Environment" from CLIR/DLF [http://www.clir.org/pubs/reports/pub110/contents.html] was published after the Digital Library Federation and the Council on Library and Information Resources commissioned Outsell, Inc., to conduct a large-scale study of undergraduates, graduate students, and faculty members at academic institutions to better understand how users' expectations of libraries are changing.

My conclusion is that if we don't remain open to changes in our users' behavior and adapt to these trends, we run the risk of becoming irrelevant. And don't think that working outside academia will enable you to avoid these changes—these young people are our future colleagues [and customers].

Teenagers and the Internet

If we want to know what's coming over the next ten years, we just have to start paying more attention to how teens are behaving in the Internet world. I love to read the Pew Internet and American Life Project reports, and their latest is a doozy.*

Teens are huge users of the Web. Duh! While it shouldn't need to be stated, it's important to remember when we are developing our five- and ten-year plans and visions that

1. All the high school-age users of our libraries are teens.
2. Within five years they will be just about all of our undergraduate student users.
3. In 10–15 years they will be the majority of the parents of the kids in our school programs.

If you're going to focus on someone to influence and have a positive view of libraries, just about every one of them is already born. If you want to design services and resources that align well with their needs and abilities, they're just not that hard to find. I live with two of these aliens myself. They're pretty neat. When I hear colleagues overtly and overly criticize this demographic, I worry they've closed their minds to understanding them.

First published in *Stephen's Lighthouse*, August 15, 2005 (http://stephenslighthouse
.sirsi.com/archives/2005/08/teenagers_and_t.html).

* Pew Internet and American Life Project, "The Internet at School," http://www
.pewinternet.org/PPF/r/163/report_display.asp. —Eds.

And the book *Everything Bad Is Good for You** presents the case that they're smarter than us older folks. Scary emerging generation gap here.

The Pew report noted that the Internet is an important (maybe critical) element in the overall educational experience of many teenagers. The widespread agreement among teens and their parents that the Internet can be a useful tool for school is driving school libraries and teachers to start building the blended learning environment (classroom and online) that supports their needs. Think about this:

1. Eighty-seven percent of all youth between the ages of 12 and 17 use the Internet. That translates into about 21 million people in the United States.

2. Of those 21 million online teens, 78 percent (or about 16 million students) say they use the Internet at school.

3. This means that 68 percent of all teenagers have used the Internet at school.

4. This represents growth of roughly 45 percent over the past four years from about 11 million teens who used the Internet in schools in late 2000 (from the 2000 Pew survey).

5. Eighteen percent of teens who use the Internet from multiple locations list school as the location where they go online most often.

6. Thirty-seven percent of teens say they believe that "too many" of their peers are using the Internet to cheat.

7. Large numbers of teens and adults have used the Web to search for information about colleges and universities. So another of the things that changed when the Internet changed everything is the dynamic of educational choices.

8. Among the other locations that teens use to go online were friends' houses (75 percent), public libraries (61 percent), and community centers (11 percent). Good news, since they can often get to library resources from outside the library—if we make them aware.

---

* Subtitled *How Today's Popular Culture Is Actually Making Us Smarter,* by Steven Johnson (New York: Riverhead, 2005). —Eds.

Millennials
My Favorite Topic

The number of teenagers using the Internet has grown 24 percent in the past four years, and 87 percent of those between the ages of 12 and 17 are online. A few highlights from the press release* are

> About 21 million teens use the Internet, and half of them say they go online every day.
>
> Fifty-one percent of online teens live in homes with broadband connections.
>
> Eighty-one percent of wired teens play games online, which is 52 percent higher than four years ago.
>
> Seventy-six percent of online teens get news online, which is 38 percent higher than four years ago.
>
> Forty-three percent have made purchases online, which is 71 percent higher than four years ago.
>
> Thirty-one percent use the Internet to get health information, which is 47 percent higher than four years ago.

This is exactly why we are doing what we're doing in libraries today with technology. We're staying in tune and in line with our users and emerging users.

First published in *Stephen's Lighthouse*, July 27, 2005 (http://stephenslighthouse.sirsi .com/archives/2005/07/millennials_my.html).

* From the Pew Internet and American Life Project, "Teens Forge Forward with the Internet and Other New Technologies," http://www.pewinternet.org/press_release .asp?r=109. —Eds.

Internet Voyeurs

The *Internet Voyeur* . . . someone who is aware of the tools, sites, and concepts of the new ways of web ecology but hasn't really experienced them personally. They've read about blogs, maybe visited a few; they've heard about, for example, MySpace and Facebook, or del.icio.us and Flickr, but only understand what they look like from afar and on an intellectual level.

Maybe one of our goals needs to be to make our colleagues and staff achieve an experiential level of learning about the potential of these new tools. Voyeurs just aren't going to be able to integrate and see the potential for innovation with these ideas. We need to provide time and support for this type of play.

First published in *Stephen's Lighthouse,* February 16, 2006 (http://stephenslighthouse .sirsi.com/archives/2006/02/Internet_voyeur.html).

What Do Teens Want?

Ah, the never-ending quandary! How to develop a site or service for teens without looking like you're pandering or uncool or worse. . . .

Joyce Valenza's NeverEnding Search blog has a good posting:*

> The most interesting question I looked at this past week asked the students how their librarian could improve the site. What is most meaningful here is that these students are not merely complaining. They know their websites and appear sincere in their desire for their growth and improvement.
>
> *Organization/Navigation:* "Some of the links don't make sense to me." "Too busy, too much stuff."
>
> *Accessibility:* "Access to e-mail and AIM." "Teach people how to use it."
>
> *Descriptions/Annotations:* "Maybe have a synopsis beneath each category to show what it is used for in case we forget." "Describe what each search tool is best for."
>
> *Documentation:* "Make the bibliographic information clearer." "Easier access to information on citing sources."

First published in *Stephen's Lighthouse,* January 4, 2006 (http://stephenslighthouse.sirsi.com/archives/2006/01/what_do_teens_w.html).

* "Teens and Virtual Libraries: The Improvements They Really Want to See," January 4, 2006, http://joycevalenza.edublogs.org/2006/01/04/teens-and-virtual-libraries-the-improvements-they-want. —Eds.

Images/Aesthetics/Fun/Teen Relevance: "Make the site more appealing." "Make it cooler looking." "It's boring." "Jazz it up." "More graphics, more color." "Flash intro, background music, links to cool bands." "More sports stuff." "I want it to say, 'Welcome [student's name here]' on the opening page."

Teacher/Project Links: "Direct links to teachers' sites."

Passwords: "Easier access from home." "An easier way to find the passwords."

Missing Content: World news/current events, more booklists, more details for English and social studies, easy links to online reference, college stuff, career stuff, government and economics, more support for research papers, and much more.

Databases: Valued, but they want "Greater variety of databases." "More contemporary databases." "Databases with scanned-in books."

Book Stuff: "Organized book lists by genre or author." "Link to the OPAC." "Book of the month, trivia on books?"

Filters and Blocking: "Let us check e-mail." (E-mail was the biggest issue!) "Have less banned websites because it makes it aggravating when you think you've found a good website for research and then you can't read it because it's blocked." "Stop blocking picture searches because students need all sorts of pictures for different projects." "Let us search for fun things."

Ephebiphobia

Ephebiphobia: "fear and loathing of teenagers." The coolest word I heard at the Collaborative Digital Reference Symposium in Denver. It came up in an interesting context. The VR (virtual reference) conversation centered around all the planning that went into launching VR services for adult users as the alpha target; and lo and behold, so much, sometimes even the majority, of the usage is coming from teens. Ewwww! They speak differently, they don't know how to ask a question, they're rude, they're abrupt, some of them are boys, etc., etc.

They're also our future. Most felt they'd learned and were really positive about their interactions with today's Millennial users. Many were acknowledging that some of their colleagues were still struggling. All in all, it was an interesting example of the unintended consequences of new technologies. And it has real implications for us as we develop portals and e-learning tools for kids, Millennials, and students if we aren't one of them.

First published in *Stephen's Lighthouse,* July 14, 2005 (http://stephenslighthouse.sirsi
.com/archives/2005/07/ephebiphobia.html).

Being Truly Teen Patron-Friendly

When I was a kid there was a bicycle rack outside the library. The library quietly made me feel welcome by providing a place to put my bike. The library and that bike rack were icons of my growing independence. I had my own bike. I had my own library card. It was something that I was proud of in that I was trusted at the library as an individual.

Recently I have been hearing too many stories about libraries thinking about (or actually doing this) restricting skateboards. What's the point of this? What do libraries want? We want positive interactions with youth so that they do well in school, respect libraries, and make them part of their lives, so that they eventually choose to vote for and support libraries as valid and valuable parts of the community. They're the folks we need to engage long-term.

So what's the point of having library staff encouraging negative teen patron interactions? Why don't we have a skateboard rack inside the library? Why would we have our patrons risk their independence if their skateboard is lost or stolen? How would they get to the library? We should support them. A skateboard box, Rubbermaid storage container, or simply a towel bar by the service desk is a simple solution that provides a service instead of a negative interaction. It's welcoming. Buy or get a secondhand old skateboard and a few sticky letters that say *welcome.* Why wouldn't we do this? It's a cheap, visible proof of welcoming attitudes.

First published in *Stephen's Lighthouse,* February 16, 2006 (http://stephenslighthouse .sirsi.com/archives/2006/02/being_truly_tee.html).

In these Olympic weeks skiers have been joined by snowboarders. At home, bicyclists have been joined by skateboarders. Time to adapt to a new reality.

We need to ask ourselves which of our policies really are not working for us and which ones need to be made positive and friendly. Let's make sure we don't extend our authority control issues with information to authoritarian control foci with users. Not good. Then let's run our policies through a discussion with our teen advisors. Adventurous and visionary libraries know the value of this through experience.

Abram doesn't forget the other end of the age spectrum. In this blog post, he highlights certain changes in the senior population.

Seniors (Instead of Millennials)

A new report from the U.S. Census Bureau, "65+ in the United States: 2005" (http://www.census.gov/Press-Release/www/releases/archives/aging_population/006544.html), covers a lot of ground. Here are the highlights from the release:

> The U.S. population age 65 and over is expected to double in size within the next 25 years. By 2030, almost one out of five Americans—some 72 million people—will be 65 years or older. The age group 85 and older is now the fastest-growing segment of the U.S. population.
>
> The health of older Americans is improving. Still, many are disabled and suffer from chronic conditions. The proportion with a disability fell significantly from 26.2 percent in 1982 to 19.7 percent in 1999. But 14 million people age 65 and older reported some level of disability in Census 2000, mostly linked to a high prevalence of chronic conditions such as heart disease or arthritis.
>
> The financial circumstances of older people have improved dramatically, although there are wide variations in income and wealth. The proportion of people aged 65 and older in poverty decreased from 35 percent in 1959 to 10 percent in 2003, mostly attributed to the support of Social Security. In 2000, the

First published in *Stephen's Lighthouse,* March 11, 2006 (http://stephenslighthouse.sirsi.com/archives/2006/03/seniors_instead.html).

poorest fifth of senior households had a net worth of US$3,500 (US$44,346 including home equity) and the wealthiest had US$328,432 (US$449,800 including home equity).

Florida (17.6 percent), Pennsylvania (15.6 percent), and West Virginia (15.3 percent) are the "oldest" states, with the highest percentages of people age 65 and older. Charlotte County, Fla. (34.7 percent), has the highest concentration of older residents and McIntosh County, N.D. (34.2 percent), ranks second.

Higher levels of education, which are linked to better health, higher income, more wealth, and a higher standard of living in retirement, will continue to increase among people 65 and older. The proportion of Americans with at least a bachelor's degree grew five-fold from 1950 to 2003, from 3.4 percent to 17.4 percent; and by 2030, more than one-fourth of the older population is expected to have an undergraduate degree. The percentage completing high school quadrupled from 1950 to 2003, from 17 percent to 71.5 percent.

As the United States as a whole grows more diverse, so does the population age 65 and older. In 2003, older Americans were 83 percent non-Hispanic white, 8 percent black, 6 percent Hispanic, and 3 percent Asian. By 2030, an estimated 72 percent of older Americans will be non-Hispanic white, 11 percent Hispanic, 10 percent black, and 5 percent Asian.

Changes in the American family have significant implications for future aging. Divorce, for example, is on the rise, and some researchers suggest that fewer children and more stepchildren may change the availability of family support in the future for people at older ages. In 1960, only 1.6 percent of older men and 1.5 percent of women age 65 and older were divorced; but by 2003, 7 percent of older men and 8.6 percent of older women were divorced and had not remarried. The trend may be continuing. In 2003, among people in their early 60s, 12.2 percent of men and 15.9 percent of women were divorced.

Like I've been saying, if you're still in the mind-set of programming for poor, web-illiterate, unhealthy folks, look again. Add to this data the impact of new retirees being Internet-aware and competent (seniors are one of the fastest-growing segments) and you've got a major shift in this market for library services.

So libraries are bookended—Millennials to the right of us, seniors to the left, and stuck in the middle with you.

(Yes, that's with apologies to Stealers Wheel: "Clowns to the left of me! Jokers to the right! Here I am stuck in the middle with you.")

Four

The Future

The Current State of Librarianship and Where It Is Going

You must have a vision of the future, or you will always be stuck in the present, over and over again.

If the Millennials are the present, what about the future? What will we

(libraries and librarians) face in the years to come?

No Librarians Left Behind

Preparing for Next-Generation Libraries (Part 1)

On January 8, 2002, President George W. Bush signed into law the No Child Left Behind Act of 2001. It redefines the federal role in K–12 education and hopes to help close the achievement gap between disadvantaged and minority students and their peers. It is based on four basic principles: stronger accountability for results, increased flexibility and local control, expanded options for parents, and an emphasis on teaching methods that have been proven to work.

A new and comprehensive report from the Canadian Coalition for School Libraries shows that students who attend schools with well-funded, well-stocked libraries managed by qualified teacher-librarians have higher achievement, improved literacy, and greater success at the postsecondary level [Ken Haycock, "The Crisis in Canada's School Libraries: The Case for Reform and Reinvestment," http://www.peopleforeducation.com/library coalition/Report03.pdf]. What's disturbing is that policymakers are ignoring the findings of literally decades of international research that show why school libraries and qualified teacher-librarians are essential components in the academic programming of any school.

What do we do? It's time to take the proverbial bull by the horns and, as library and learning specialists, anticipate future student and school needs and future (and current) technologies "in the service of learning."

From *Multimedia and Internet@Schools* 10, no. 6 (November–December 2003): 6–8. Published first by Information Today, Inc. (http://www.infotoday.com). Reprinted with permission. All rights reserved.

THE KEYS TO SUCCESS
FOR NO CHILD LEFT BEHIND TO BE SUCCESSFUL, NO LIBRARIAN OR LIBRARY RESOURCE CAN BE LEFT BEHIND, EITHER!

In our libraries, as librarians, teachers, technicians, multimedia specialists, and as learners ourselves, we have adapted fairly well to the changes of the past ten years—the hardware, the Internet, CD-ROM, variant e-mail systems, educational software, the Web, portals, networks, e-books, multiple search engines, and blended approaches to the invisible Web, the public Web, and licensed products, as well as new book paradigms. Many of these trends will have a *greater* impact than the Web has had on society in the past decade! The web stuff was a mere acorn compared to the oak of change coming down the pipeline.

As a futurist, I have developed a keen eye for identifying those trends that will make a difference. As librarians and educators, we can make a difference over the next five years by understanding what's coming, learning how it works, seeking key benefits for our students, and becoming the resource in our schools that lifts our learners up to their full potential.

❚ What will search and find look like in the next 3–5 years?

❚ What will the Web look like?

❚ What end-user devices will be popular?

❚ What will our learning and work environments be?

❚ What are our school library microtrends?

SEARCH, FIND, AND DISPLAY

Until now, the web search engines were pretty much word searchers that searched inverted indexes and, more recently, applied relevancy algorithms to their results instead of the less-than-satisfying alphabetical or chronological results lists of olden times. These were just ranked lists and pointers to resources.

Take a look at some of these recent newcomers and how they've changed the face of search. Do users need training anymore? Do they need intermediaries or search coaches? Yes, they surely do—but we need to understand it, too.

These search engines have different ways of adding value to search. Some do it through insights into the nature of "discovery," and some just display the results better for quicker access. The focus of the search engine designer has moved from the search box and algorithms to making results display more usefully on a basic learning level.

So one major trend in search is to create a visual display that looks like a map, or folders, or a solar system, or some other metaphor that shows you the relationships and dimensionality of the information in the content—derived from the internal taxonomies, thesauri, or proprietary algorithms. This is very interesting and has a great deal of potential. Playing with these new-style search and display services will provide insights into where and how our current students will be exploring the Web next.

The other major trend is not to just visually map a search result but to organize the hits, and not just public web hits. These tools can often be licensed and tuned to our intranets, OPACs, and invisible web resources. Sometimes these look like folders that mirror the metadata in the source, and sometimes they create metadata on the fly through sources they choose. Some just look like editorially (human) organized links, but they're not.

Our beloved Google had better evolve and adapt, too. We're already seeing Google offering a multitude of new services (and ads) that index and serve up many information formats besides the traditional HTML, as well as loads of new additions, including some media and beyond-PDF options. Some of these aren't just text—a peek into the multimedia future. As librarians who train students and others to search, we have a critical role to teach budding searchers how to choose the right resource.

Are we ready for multimedia searching? As more and more valuable but non-text information is stored and accessible via the Web, we'd better be. In the new music search engines—some pretty amazing stuff here, too—we see the potential to tap into words buried in streaming sound. Are you ready to search full-motion digital video in DVDs?

Are we ready for multilingual searching? How about being able to easily search other languages when buried and wrapped in a picture or graphic? A lot is happening in this space.

WHAT'S NEXT FOR THE WEB?

We're entering an era in which the databases are going to get even more massive. The role of information literacy training will grow, not diminish, with the coming generations of learners. Being computer literate is not information literacy. The issues of finding (not just searching) both the visible and the invisible Web will challenge our schools, our learners, and our society in coming years.

It's becoming clear that the search "problem" on the Web may end up being solved by some solutions that resemble PC games more than what we see today, navigating a three-dimensional space using such currently crude tools as joysticks, gloves, and eyeball goggles!

The next-generation, but by no means final, architecture of the Internet and Web is already here. You can see this in the file-sharing (so-called P2P or peer-to-peer) protocols that don't require web pages or HTML to share information or any digital objects (images, documents, whole websites, records, learning nuggets, etc.). Peer architecture is closely related to things that are near and dear to our library hearts—full-text, full-image, and full-article delivery.

In this presentation to medical librarians, Abram and Jane Dysart described where they saw library technology applications in the near future.

Re-creating Services with New Technologies

Service Strategies for the Millennium

Stephen Abram and Jane Dysart

Use technology to help users by

> Providing easy access to catalogs, indexes, special collections, e-books and e-journals, websites, web collections, maps, images, and sound, licensed content such as databases and e-collections, experts, and even to librarians for assistance and guidance

> Training users in computer literacy, in Internet skills, in information literacy

> Selecting and directing users to the best websites, "safe" sites for kids, and patient (consumer health) information

> Providing services to businesses: customized research, answers, and reports; virtual reference and distance services; information advice and analysis

> Providing competitive intelligence by watching, analyzing, extrapolating, recommending, and interpreting

> Partnering to integrate public and university collections, to support curriculum by having librarians teaching information segments of courses, to leverage special collections between educators and cultural groups, to ally libraries and businesses in activities such as clinical trials, and to develop intranets and knowledge management initiatives

From a presentation given to the Medical Library Association, Ottawa, Ontario, October 2004.

Enable knowledge sharing in our organizations by

    Focusing on clients

    Focusing on faculty and students

    Focusing on content

    Focusing on connections

    Focusing on point of need

While I'm Thinking about It . . .

We've got a bunch of specialized search engines:

1. In Yahoo we can search Creative Commons content at http://search.yahoo.com/cc/. We can do the same in Google at http://www.google.com/advanced_search/.
2. We can search U.S. government sites at http://firstgov.gov.
3. I can search university and college sites alone at http://www.google.com/options/universities.html.
4. I can search a lot of public blogs at http://blogsearch.google.com.
5. I can limit by domain and country.

Some topical searches are possible, but I am always getting questions like this:

1. What public libraries have cool audiobook/talking book sites?
2. What are the interesting kids' sites? Anyone doing online story hours?
3. What are the best ideas in teen sites?
4. What's working for seniors now?
5. Who's doing innovative stuff in virtual book clubs?

First published in *Stephen's Lighthouse,* December 28, 2005 (http://stephenslighthouse.sirsi.com/archives/2005/12/while_im_thinki_1.html).

Soooo—*Why can't I search the content of all North American (or international) public library sites in one place?* I'm not talking about their catalogs or Open WorldCat (http://www.oclc.org/worldcat/open/default.htm). I mean their pages. How do we easily find all the cool stuff that public libraries have done?

Am I missing something somewhere? Does this exist already? It seems like such a useful thing for library website developers, owners, and strategists to have. Could someone create a targeted harvest using a list of URLs? Then we could share best practices, get better more quickly, allow innovation to diffuse more quickly, build on success . . . seems like a no-brainer.

No Librarians Left Behind
Preparing for Next-Generation Libraries (Part 2)

WHAT DEVICES ARE COMING DOWN THE PIKE?

First, I think it's pretty clear that within five years the PC will not be the dominant electronic tool, or even access device. Clearly laptops outsell desktops now, and handheld devices outsell both. We are seeing increasing use of flat screens. This isn't just about saving space on desktops. It's about moving products, services, and information to where the users are, which means we will see screens appearing on our freezer doors, refrigerators, microwaves, walls, countertops, and desks. Imagine what it will mean to libraries when screens are paper-thin and can be applied anywhere—even on our book stacks!

Wireless is another obvious trend that many libraries are adapting to very quickly. Some schools are trapped in buildings that limit their technological flexibility. It's just too expensive to wire through poured concrete, asbestos, urea formaldehyde, or historically important buildings. Many institutions have already discovered that such technological approaches as wireless SkyPort drops and Bluetooth solutions can work around these limits cost-effectively, strongly enhancing service and access.

Besides the current penetration of the kid market with cell phones and pagers, we see the proliferation of Palm Pilots, BlackBerries, WorldPhones, and DoCoMo devices worldwide. Indeed, it's a rare new PCS digital phone

From *Multimedia and Internet@Schools* 11, no. 1 (January–February 2004): 17–19. Published first by Information Today, Inc. (http://www.infotoday.com). Reprinted with permission. All rights reserved.

that doesn't come with, or have options for, MP3 players, radio, browsers, e-mail, streaming media TV, or voice recognition. Text messaging is increasing in popularity worldwide.

Some libraries are supporting nomadic computing in recognition that this is where their users are heading, seeing this as an opportunity to improve service. Mount Sinai Hospital library in Toronto has made the wireless plunge and offers many key databases available through doctors' and other health professionals' Palm Pilots at the bedside. Information now truly needs to be where the users' decisions are, not where they have to go.

Voice recognition is almost ready for prime time. Many of us use it when we call 411 and give our answer to the computer's query, "What city please?" It doesn't take a genius to see this turning any telephone into a speak-search-and-read-it-to-me device, especially since no one wants to use the telephone button pad as an interface.

LEARNING AND WORK ENVIRONMENTS

This is probably the area of biggest change. For years we've been following the technological advance we've termed "convergence." That's pretty well over; now the challenge will be to converge the content, librarian services, and technology into our learners' context—moving library services to *where* they need it, not just when.

We can call this new environment a "collaboratory"—a blended and overlapping thinking, decision-making, and learning environment. Adding librarian tricks (collaborative digital reference, virtual reference libraries, virtual teams, and shared portals) to the bricks and clicks will be the goal. This goes beyond virtual classrooms, chat rooms, and videoconferences. It's about communities of interest and communities of practice, and it's also about e-neighborhoods. We're moving to a world where sharing and integrated, cooperative partnerships will be the norm. These partnerships are developing between teachers, teacher-librarians, school boards, parents, vendors, and curriculum professionals. Libraries have been on the edge of some of these trends as we have developed statewide consortial licensing and services. We're looking at a new way of working, and a new environment into which the services of librarians and researchers can be offered.

Another key trend is e-learning—Internet-enabled learning, a blended learning environment in which classroom instruction (virtual and live) and distance education courses are combined with e-learning that intersperses live interactions and learning nuggets delivered in appropriate time frames—asynchronously and asymmetrically—to the right work and study environments. If libraries are not integrated into the new blended learning environment, then we will lose relevance to the mainstream of society and education. Our teaching, selection, collection, and service development skills will serve us well in this new environment of buying, supporting, and introducing electronic courseware.

SCHOOL LIBRARY MICROTRENDS

There are loads of opportunities in the library sector. One of the biggest is what is being called virtual reference or collaborative digital reference services. This is the ability to provide online remote service. This can be as simple as an "Ask a librarian . . . live!" button on your OPAC or library site, web-based Q&A cafés, or a real-time, live-chat homework helper service. We can certainly see the day when school libraries will, of necessity, have to keep online "homework helper" hours through instant messaging, virtual reference tools, or (sadly) e-mail.

We are definitely seeing cool developments in e-book management systems. We're seeing large collections that are actually tied to MARC records, allowing seamless integration into our OPACs. We are all reminded of our professional role as library workers to protect freedom of expression, and patron rights to equity of access with privacy and intellectual freedom. We're suddenly "important" and "informed" on issues that the power brokers and money folks care about.

The strategic window for opportunity for librarians is huge, but keep in mind that it won't be open long. We're about to enter the Boomer retirement era. It will be the largest flight of knowledge capital from the open market in history. *Knowledge*—tacit, explicit, and cultural—will need to be transferred, not just information. The gauntlet has been thrown down for librarianship. Use the technology, use our professional skills, learn from others, and we will be so stupendously successful that the world will beat a path to our (virtual) door!

While our foundation is in content of every sort, our essence, our value, and our vision have always been about context. We lift our eyes up and look to see how we take our building blocks—brick, clicks, and tricks—and apply them in the context of our society, students, and institutions. We build better learners. We underpin a better, freer democracy. We ensure the long-term success of our institutions. We help students, inventors, artists, writers, and researchers create the future. Remember this as we step forward to meet the challenges we encounter along this adventure we call librarianship.

So it's quite simple, really. If we keep our eye on the future and focus on the learner's needs, *no librarian will be left behind.*

In this detailed and artistic piece, Abram demonstrated accurate foresight in 1999 of technological changes in the current millennium. Some of his predictions (for example, offshoot issues surrounding computer system Y2K compliance efforts) have passed already. Some of the changes still await us in 2007.

Shift Happens

Ten Key Trends in Our Profession and Ten Strategies for Success

INTRODUCTION

I once watched a robin build her nest from what was available around my yard. Her choices were interesting. She had lots of material to choose from, but kept picking up the shiny, silver tinsel from our discarded skeleton of a Christmas tree. Her nest was beautiful when done. It was also more cold, and non-absorbent, and she was never able to successfully get her eggs to hatch. One of the morals of this story: sometimes that which we find attracts us is not necessarily what's best for the purpose. Perhaps adopting the latest shiny technologies for our libraries and users isn't the best way to incubate knowledge and encourage the best behaviors in either society or organizations.

Let's learn from our past experiences. For example, we can ask ourselves that if one of the real end-user benefits of the information-based CD-ROM is its portability, then how portable are the CDs in library collections? Usually (but not always) there's precious little portability left after a library has got hold of these resources. And when we look to DVD to solve our problems with the limited storage capacity of CD, we still hit walls. DVD may be a possible solution, but it's unlikely to succeed. We could acknowledge that the long-term trend is that Moore's Law of storage capacity has not been transferred to bandwidth. Why then would

First published simultaneously in *Serials Librarian* 38, nos. 1–2 (2000): 41–59; and *From Carnegie to Internet2: Forging the Serials Future,* ed. P. Michelle Fiander, Joseph C. Harmon, and Jonathan David Makepeace (Binghamton, NY: Haworth, 2000), 41–59.

we want to invest heavily in an emerging technology like DVD, which will be surpassed by distant server-based products, which can be updated more frequently and enjoy equal performance? Indeed, the entire DVD technology has been driven by the needs of movies over much else—in the same way that CD-ROM was driven by the needs of music. Wiring may drive bandwidth, but does anyone actually believe that the cable, copper, and glass fiber-wiring infrastructure so conscientiously built over the past century will survive the onslaught of high-bandwidth, wireless technologies? Whither CD-ROM in the world of cheap or free lap/palm-tops wirelessly connected to the next-generation web infrastructure through wireless links? Add to this the strong trend toward enterprise and consortium content acquisition, where information users can opt in to several pools of content through membership, enrollment, or employment, and you have the knowledge-based society, seamlessly connected to oceans of information with no need to consider alternative delivery formats. Are libraries well prepared to deal with more change and more changing technologies, and is there better positioning for the skills of librarians and information-access professionals?

Rushing to adopt shiny new technologies may do nothing to forward librarians or institutions toward our goals. Of course, we can still see a secure place for CD in the future, and the transitional technologies of special drives and towers will bridge the gap. However, some library technology trends are emerging as we move into the next phase of our future. We need to acknowledge from our learning with CD-ROM experiences that long-term technological stability is a chimera. For those of us who build our library's technology and services, we find that we must be mindful of the global trends or we may back ourselves into a corner, far from the mainstream of society. Below are some of my thoughts on current trends. Some may not be the most important trends, since *shift happens*—but they're what's occupying my thoughts today, and I want to explore in this article what impact they may have on marketing our libraries, our technology, and ourselves. There is a distinct emphasis below on making the nest warm and not going for the shiny stuff too fast.

TRENDS

Trend No. 1: The Pace of Change Is Too Slow!

At a recent conference of information industry CEOs, the executives said that their biggest challenge was that they felt their organizations were "boldness challenged." They explicitly felt that they weren't introducing change *fast enough*! They felt that their organizations needed to adopt more modern team strategies to involve customers in the process of rapid change, which accompanies most products of the information industry. Such involvement, the CEOs thought, would engender trust between the information industry and its clients. In the information industry, speed is an issue, and the introduction of continuous change in products and services is the norm.

What does this mean to us? Well, for one, it means that the products and services we market to our clients and users are likely to mutate from day to day in both small and big ways. The ability of suppliers and purchasers to communicate these changes quickly and broadly will be difficult, if not impossible. The days of having years between Dialog I and Dialog II, or a year or more between new releases/updates of CD-ROM software are gone. Monthly and daily updates, and changes and improvements to interfaces, content, and terms are likely and, often, desirable. Web culture not only encourages rapid change; it often demands it as a cultural precept of the new knowledge society. This presents us with some real challenges.

Trend No. 2: Education Is Out—Learning Is In

When did we stop calling it learning? Think about it in terms of technology and marketing. Education is something done "to" people, while learning is something that people do for themselves. Indeed, in many ways technology is something we also do "to" people.

When I think about marketing our technology in the "learning" context rather than in a systems or content context, I start to think about marketing a learning environment. Marketing the environment, and making the technology and content secondary, highlights what librarians create rather than making us shills for the products we purchase. We create learning environments, and anything that doesn't enhance learning or gets in the way of learning is "bad." This perspective can drive training and orientation strategies that are holistic and based in long-term literacy skills, rather than being purely training for individual applications and products. It also makes choices related to content and interfaces easier to make.

Trend No. 3: The Next Generation Is Largely Composed of Nextheads

Librarians usually are not nextheads; we tend to be textheads. We all know that physical books stopped dominating in or around 1990 in terms of revenue and unit sales. Today the printed text represents only a small fraction of all stored data and information, and in some markets like business, it represents a very small portion of content acquisition budgets. However, deemphasizing text has driven a further change that we need to explicitly acknowledge—the dominance of educated persons who decode and internalize "text" well is ending.

Recognizing that there are many different kinds and mixes of intelligence and learning styles, we need to be aware that text-based collection development is becoming just one tool for serving our emerging markets well. Many libraries use software like iKIOSK and Fortres to ensure that information applications like e-mail, chat, multimedia, Real-Audio, RealVideo, streaming video, and more are not accessible on public access terminals. This policy ensures that only "serious" applications are available without compromising system performance. As we move into the future, we'll have to remember that information will be coming in many ways, and our traditional preference and respect for text-based information will need to be reviewed and balanced with the market's needs. The rule of introducing these emerging technologies is to match the technology to the user's needs and styles—not the provider's or intermediary's comfort level.

Trend No. 4: The Next Generation Is What It Needs to Be and Nothing Less

As it ages, each generation develops a culture of generational doom. In ancient Greece, Socrates bemoaned the lack of respect the younger generation had for learning; and Shakespeare wrote: "Thou has most traitorously corrupted the youth of the realm in erecting a grammar school" [*King Henry VI,* Part II, act 4, scene 7]. The coming generations will have been trained through many means to adapt information differently. Think computer games. Players' ability to enter a "problem set" virtually and solve the problem through multivariate paths, stored clues, and information prepares them well for entering bodies of "information" with problems to solve and decisions to make using three-dimensional interfaces. Play Zelda, Myst, or whatever and you'll know what I mean. Apply the same navigation paradigm to a file of spreadsheets and it's amazing what insights can emerge. Topographic-style interfaces like Cartia, while at first causing a level of discomfort, actually allow the user to enter an unknown body of information in a thoughtful way. In marketing technologies, we need to acknowledge our own prejudices and then respect the fact that the clients' abilities may be informed in a way ours are not.

Trend No. 5: Change Cannot Be Managed Generationally Anymore

Change now cycles in a hamster's life span—less than three years. In this environment, we can't expect the education system to prepare fully formed leaders, employees, and citizens for the future—it just can't.

For one, anyone who has successfully completed a program of study is back at square one in about five years, unless, of course, they have developed a habit or predilection for continuous learning. For another, the

Boomers are figuratively this "pig in the snake," by which I mean they represent demographically a big clump of workers needing regular retreading on a very large scale. As marketers of technology combined with content and an environment for learning, we are well tooled and equipped to be the gurus for the "knowledge ecology." Someone needs to ensure that the environment for continuous learning is managed well. But this is not enough. Someone also needs to communicate that this resource exists to ensure that people remain successful. This will be a key role of information professionals—to create awareness of the impact that can be made on the individual who participates in the information environments we create.

Trend No. 6: Virtual Is a Place, Not a Format

Perception is reality—if you believe something exists, then you will act on that belief. Generally, most adults cannot separate belief from perception. It is clear that for information professionals and librarians, "virtuality" will dominate as an environment. Many consumers in our markets now believe that information is free, that everything's on the Web, and that physical access to any information of value is now possible from home in your pajamas. The role of marketing, and the sacred trust for professional librarians, is that we must begin to introduce the truth about this situation to our users, and, sometimes, our decision makers. If we don't, we run the risk of allowing a massively transformational technology like the World Wide Web to actually decrease intelligence in society. We run the risk of encouraging a new Dark Age. Previous transformational technologies have been the telephone and television. I leave it up to you to decide if their introduction increased intelligence in society or not. Are we serving our enterprises or society by simply championing AltaVista or Edgar, for example, at the desktop?

Trend No. 7: Communities of Interest Are No Longer Bounded by Geography

Most institutional structures will evolve, but many will disappear. If you define yourself or your role in the context of your institutions (university libraries, public libraries, community information centers) without a strong understanding and communication of your role in that environment, then your position and place are at risk. In marketing terms, focus your efforts on what you can do well and sacrifice the benign, the inadequate, or the unaffordable. For example, the emerging strong trend toward distance education will not destroy every traditional educational institution but it will hurt some; new organizations will emerge while others will disappear. The role of some libraries as community centers will decline if people find networks of like-minded individuals through the Web to which they have stronger ties than those they have to their local neighborhoods. If you rely on proximity or word of mouth for your marketing and you can foresee that your community is no longer tied together through proximity, then carefully review your marketing strategies.

Trend No. 8: New Brands Are Emerging on the Web

One e-newsletter announced that Amazon, Drudge, and Yahoo were the newest major brands created by the Web. There are other new content brands emerging too. What is worrisome, however, is that the traditional value-added publishers and aggregators, as they reinvent themselves for the "New World Order," run some risks. First, traditional supporters may permanently or temporarily abandon them, destroying their business models. Some content publishers may not be around by the time the lusty new, and possibly free, web services are found to be lacking for serious research and decision support.

As for marketing a professional library, what does it say about a library that offers access through simple hyperlinking to Internet resources, just the normal stuff any patron can likely get at home anyway? If librarians are purveyors of access to free and shallow web resources, how does that present us over the long term? In marketing language, the library's client value proposition (what value your clients actually place on your services) has always been highest for selected access to deep information and information of high quality. As the world of information shifts, you have to be able to prove to your clients that you actually have something that they can't get elsewhere more cheaply. Web links to the usual Internet resources won't cut it. Can you prove that your services are differentiated in a visible, tangible way from the web experiences they have at home on their computers, which, by the way, are more than likely better than anything available in your library? When you know the answer to this question, you know what you've got that's valuable to them.

Trend No. 9: Extra Pre-millennium Work Is Stifling Change

The infamous Y2K bug is a double-edged sword. On the one hand, it is stifling change and new product introduction as programming resources are shifted to reengineer old products and system architectures. Most companies have had periods of lockdown in order to test for Y2K compliance and readiness. This has taken resources, analysis time, and funding away from developing new products and services and improving others.

On the other hand, Y2K has promoted change, namely, the opportunity to replace legacy equipment and programs with new hardware and software. The result of this mass upgrading will be the most homogenous technical environment in decades. After the turn of the century, some institutions will likely continue to struggle with dated technology, but for the most part, the environment will be greatly improved. I also anticipate the new millennium will see the largest introduction of new, and primarily web-based, applications ever seen.

What does this mean for marketing a library's services? Training for both librarians and clients becomes one where understanding certain basics (Windows, browsers, etc.) will give the ultimate searcher a leg up. Application of content training in the absence of an understanding of the technological environment will fail. Marketing your training services will move to this environment as well—pop-up ads or click-through features leading the end user to their learning goal will cease being only the domain of for-profit entities and will be used to communicate tips, library training events, and library news. It will be equally important to focus on teaching end users *finding* skills, while reserving the advanced *searching* skills for information professionals.

Trend No. 10: Every Profession's Relevance Is in Question

As librarians and information professionals, we agonize that our value as a profession is in a state of flux. Focus groups with librarians and information managers tell us that there is one overriding concern—sustaining *relevance* to our organizations in an era of constant and transformational change. This is not a matter affecting just our profession. Indeed, the Web has changed the way many professions and companies conduct business. I believe that the marketing tack for librarians to take is to return to two fundamental principles: understand the difference between intellectual and physical access; and market the librarian, not the technology.

First, we need to remember the important difference between *intellectual* and *physical* access. As librarians, we can very successfully compete on *intellectual* access activities like information coaching, training, and problem definition (remember reference interviewing!). Over the coming years it will be more and more difficult to position our sense of place in terms of physical access. Our role as information counselors will increase as the information "appliance" becomes the norm and wireless and bandwidth advances destroy any advantage of CD or DVD collections, multimedia software, and full motion and sound services.

Second, we need to understand fully the role we play in adding value to information experiences. Unlike those few remaining bank tellers, we are not in the transaction and delivery business. Since the invention of the photocopier and other delivery technologies, we have run the risk of marketing ourselves in terms of faster and speedier delivery. But emphasizing speed neglects the key, but largely intangible, role we play in the transfer of knowledge and the creation of environments for successful intellectual capital growth. We have marketed the dickens out of the latest in new technologies and have lost ground to a certain degree. We need to get back to basics by marketing the librarian, not the technology.

BACK TO THE BIRD'S NEST

Now back to our robin and her nest. The robin is us. The nest is our library environment. The robin built a beautiful nest using the latest, most available, and most appealing materials. But she forgot what the nest was for in the first place—to incubate the next generation to become successful participants in the ecology. PCs in libraries are meaningless without money for content and staff. The content is useless if it's not both physically and intellectually accessible. The staff programs are pointless if they're not aimed at increasing knowledge and learning. Market the hell out of that idea—not shiny technology.

STRATEGIES FOR SUCCESS

Before we start to think about what strategies we must undertake to be successful in the new age we must acknowledge one fact: the Information Era failed. It failed miserably. The "information highway" metaphor is no longer useful. It's worse than drinking water through a fire hose to receive all the information we need, all the time, anywhere! Our beloved users actually drowned as we shoved more and more information down the highway—just because it was there. We were laying roads without a map and quickly discovered that new metaphors were needed. Information isn't about traveling down a road and stopping to pick some up at predefined intersections and towns. That's a telephone or cable TV model, and it serves the interests of those industries dependent on wire and heedless of the coming wireless environment. Information is an immersion environment, and the metaphor of "information oceans," not an "information highway," will redirect us as we define the future information environment and our roles in it.

We are entering the *Knowledge Era.* This is a post-Information Age where the competitive advantage moves from information access to knowledge creation, from physical access to intellectual access. The successful services and knowledge objects will be products, enterprises, and environments designed for precognition and adaptation. As you enter the Knowledge Era, your focus must go from achieving stability to continuous redefinition and reinvention, while being comfortable with ambiguity and sustained chaos. "To react is to fail; to anticipate is to succeed." We already see this in the faster cycle time for change and iteration—the compression of the concept-through-action continuum. Simply put, the world of right answers and facts gives way to consensus answers and informed guesses. It's the difference between learning history through memorizing dates and understanding history through synthesizing multiple viewpoints and scenarios.

As we enter the Knowledge Era, we move from the old Information Era, where the gurus were those who understood the technology nuts and bolts, to one where the gurus are those who understand and communicate innovation in a future context. Information combined with insight rules. Interestingly, we see the supply-and-demand model of economics falling apart in the knowledge ecology as we move to one where supply *drives* demand. The value-added, and therefore economically valuable, activities are filtering, selection, organizing, digesting, packaging, and just plain dealing with the flood of information.

Strategy No. 1 for Success: Know the Difference between Data, Information, and Knowledge, and Also Know That These Distinctions Are Not Enough!

Wisdom is not the end result one seeks in society. Our goal in the knowledge-based sector is to integrate the data-information-knowledge continuum in order to fundamentally and positively impact *behavior* in our enterprises and society.

Data is raw facts with no context and no inherent meaning. Data only have value to end users in context; data professionals can add this value by applying standards such as SGML, HTML, fields, tags, and MARC; by normalizing data; and through quality control.

Information is the tangible representation of data within a specific context. In order for information to be successful, it must be useful. To be useful it must be communicated to a user and must meet the specific needs of this user. Librarians and other information professionals can add value to information by representing data and content effectively.

Knowledge is information in context. For knowledge to exist there must be congruity between the information and the individual's context. Knowledge can only be stored in a human being. Knowledge cannot be stored on paper or in a computer; only information and data can be stored in this way.

Behavior can be thought of as simply "decisions" that result in action, even if that action is non-action. Enterprises exist to provide an ecology for decision making. The key success factor is intelligent, informed results that have value in proportion to the results required to meet the needs of the individual or social organization. Keeping this principle in mind, your desired strategy must be to focus your service goals on having an impact on personal and organizational behaviors and only on those behaviors which will have a strategic impact. To put it bluntly, if you focus on managing information or managing knowledge with your information skills, you will not succeed as well as you might like. If having a bunch of knowledgeable people and lots of information were power, universities would be at the top of the economic food chain. They are not. To be successful in an enterprise you must focus your information services, collections, and strategies on the most desired and strategically important *behaviors* in your organization. Our lesson for the millennium is that information is not enough.

Strategy No. 2 for Success: Spend More Time and Money on People Issues Than on Technology Issues

Spend time on markets (customers, clients, users, and students) over infrastructure. Don't focus more time on organization structure and processes than you do on market dynamics and behaviors.

Know your stakeholders. Determine your client's psychographic profile. The *Dilbert* team (The Boss, Dilbert, Catbert, Dogbert, Ratbert, Wally, and Alice) is a fun way to help visualize and understand client needs. If that doesn't work for you, use *The Simpsons* or study the advertising literature for demographic profile inventories. It's not important to be perfectly right; it is important to start focusing on the market and the maps and reduce the focus on your own navel. Focus on your *knowledge workers,* since they hold the organization's memory and competencies. They have talents and knowledge that are underexploited in the enterprise, and this knowledge leaves the building in the elevator every night. Look for underexploited knowledge and then look for synergies between knowledge pools.

Strategy No. 3 for Success: Understand That People Are Different and Not Like You

Diversity is the norm, not the exception. Learn about learning from such great thinkers as Gardner, Bloom, and Piaget. A powerful tool for developing learning strategies is the Taxonomy of Intelligence and Learning Styles. [See Howard Gardner, *Intelligence Reframed: Multiple Intelligences for the 21st Century* (New York: Basic Books, 1999).] It identifies seven key learning styles that are present in all people in different combinations and proportions:

1. *Visual/Spatial is picture smart.* People with this intelligence can think in images and pictures and develop clear visual images and representations.

2. *Verbal/Linguistic is word smart.* Their talent is to think in words, with highly developed auditory skills.

3. *Musical/Rhythmic is music smart.* They think in sounds, rhythms, and patterns and sing, hum, and whistle to themselves.

4. *Logical/Mathematical is number smart.* These people think conceptually and are skilled in reasoning, logic, and problem-solving.

5. *Bodily/Kinesthetic is body smart.* These people can process knowledge through bodily sensation and have excellent fine-motor coordination.

6. *Interpersonal is people smart.* They think and process information by relating, cooperating, and communicating with others.

7. *Intrapersonal is self-smart.* They are skilled in inner focusing and display a strong personality.

Acknowledge that there is more than one learning style. Don't indulge yourself with a strategy that assumes others learn the way you do. An effective strategy accommodates the diverse ways in which humans learn and adapt information. Focus on people and their diversity and you will be more successful than if you focus on an ideal, model user.

Strategy No. 4 for Success: Seek the Understandable, Not the Intuitive

There is no single best interface, and "intuitive" is a word for fools. If we accept the proposition that people learn in an innumerable combination of fashions, then there will be an unlimited range of potential versions of intuitive. Search out the understandable and learnable interface—not the illusory intuitive one. By focusing on an actual interface, your evaluation will be based in reality and you will develop realistic criteria. Some interface design and evaluation principles here are

1. You must design interfaces for humans. Humans come in many cultural types, with various levels of information literacy and different learning behaviors. Tune the interface to the full range of users or, ideally, allow users to tune them themselves.

2. Be prepared to adapt your interface continuously. You will discover many improvements as you go along—test and launch regularly—and don't keep dozens in a bucket to launch en masse.

3. Tunable interfaces for now probably mean tiers—like basic, advanced, professional, etc. Watch for interfaces in the future that learn and adapt based on user behavior.

4. Understand that *search* is not equal to *find*. Librarians love searching and the thrill of the hunt. End users hate searching and want to find information. Evaluating a "search" interface for end users

solely on its searching ability puts the analysis in the wrong court. Evaluate its ability to quickly produce satisfying answers.

5. Support the full information continuum—identification through analysis with visible value-add. An interface that merely delivers results or answers without making it easily adaptable to the user's workflow and needs is not optimal. Recognize that we need to know what happens to the information after it leaves the service. For example, providing a comprehensive pile of annual reports on paper is nice. But if the user must enter those numbers into a spreadsheet, we have merely provided data; we have not added value where the user could import the data into a spreadsheet.

6. Determine how you can formally integrate internal and external information. Can your users really tell the difference? Can you place the same interfaces on top of both, thus reducing the interface learning barrier?

7. Is the intranet an extension of the library, or is the library an extension of the intranet? There is no right answer to this question, but you really should choose one focus. This is the "enterprise portal" question, where you need to decide if information access is an enterprise-wide issue or a departmental one.

8. Build products and services that highlight the relevance of the librarian/information professional. The role of the librarian should be explicit, tangible, and accessible from all knowledge products. Are "you" in your interface? How easy is it to find "you" from your portal?

9. Focusing on the understandable forces you to clearly strategize in the areas of understanding—training, support, and communication. Interfaces must be understandable and as easy to train for as possible—calling them "intuitive" trivializes the role of librarians.

10. Manage meaning, not content. Content doesn't need strong management (it's generally managed by the content providers). Meaning is what librarians do well in interpreting resources for users. Content in context (*meaning*) is the goal.

Strategy No. 5 for Success: Understand the Real Needs of Your Market and the Individuals Therein

Many enterprises base their future success on either targeting future markets (those kids growing up now) or being a part of the process of teaching the future generation (schools, colleges, and universities). It is common for older generations to understand the next generation poorly. This lack of a complete understanding of one's "market" drives poor decision making.

Focus on Generation "J," the "Joystick Generation." If you're thinking that keyboards will represent the primary interface to your information products in the next decade for this multi-literate group, you're fooling yourself and fundamentally misunderstanding their skills and competencies. Watch for voice response technologies to outpace keyboards faster than predicted. Make your investments where it allows respect for the nexthead skills they embody. Does your OPAC strategy allow for multimedia, chat rooms, and streaming video, or have you limited your future by "saving" money with lower-grade PCs? Irony rules here, as the generations move through the future together, yet apart.

Strategy No. 6 for Success: Understand the Dynamics of Your Ecology

Ecology is the science of understanding whole environments. To focus on our ecology is to focus on human-centered information management. Therefore, the relationships of the parts to the whole are of paramount importance. In order to effectively help people adapt information, you must immerse yourself in their information ocean; i.e., understand your "user." The shift we're experiencing right now is a refreshing move from a technology-centered focus, with the emphasis on generation, collection, and distribution, to one where the emphasis is on effective use and usefulness. The ecology is "sick" if there is not a balance between technology and people.

Strategically look at your ecology and your role in it.

1. View and map the relationships.
2. How is learning happening, and with what?
3. When do innovation and creativity occur?
4. How do they turn ideas into action?

Strategy No. 7 for Success: Understand the Rule of 15 Percent and Apply It in Your Development and Evaluations

There is a significant body of research about human perception that hypothesizes that humans can only see change when it is visible and when it exceeds 12–15 percent. This has been tested on such diverse subjects as candlelight, music volume, added-value features, price, and job evaluation points. It used to be said that you could be successful if you did 100 things 1 percent better; the 15-percent theory would postulate that, in such an environment, no one would notice that. This theory reinforces the role of strategy in setting as priorities those things and activities that really matter. Priorities for libraries should be proving to the user (actually prove!)

the visible value in your products, services, and organization; and assessing whether parts of your service are at risk of commoditization—that is, services that can no longer be improved with added-value features. Interlibrary loan, for example, may be at risk of commoditization since web services such as Northern Light and Electric Library offer similar services.

Strategy No. 8 for Success: Be Realistic about the Adoption Cycle

The future of information professionals will be integrally tied to introducing new services, interfaces, content, products, and training to the enterprise. Each "new" thing will need to be adopted by the users and markets. Understand three classic laws of adoption:

1. There are five immutable adoption stages that *every* individual must progress through before completing the adoption: awareness, interest, evaluation, trial, adoption. Failure to follow these steps, in order, will result in the failure of users to adopt a new idea, product, or service.

2. There are five key attributes that favor more *rapid* adoption. Feel free to ensure your initiative uses these in a Machiavellian manner. These attributes are relative advantage, compatibility, reduced complexity, trial-ability, and observability.

3. There is a classic bell curve to adoption and the individual's pattern of risk-taking behaviors:

Innovators	2.5 percent
Early adopters	13 percent
Early majority	17 percent
Middle majority	34 percent
Laggards	17.5 percent
Non-adopters	16 percent

Don't be fooled about the value of your initiative by the reactions of late adopters during the launch period. Also, don't get too encouraged by innovators' excitement until you get some feedback from the second-stage early adopters. New initiatives are exciting. Don't let your strategies fail by evaluating them too early.

Strategy No. 9 for Success: Truly Know That People Don't Want or Need Information

This may seem like librarian heresy, but people don't want information—especially in the form of articles, books, printouts, fiche, diskettes, websites, or whatever. They want usable answers, confidence, and success. They want to *find,* not *search.* With this insight you can be prepared to market to your users' real needs. We've spent decades marketing our collections and services and not vastly increasing our success. By targeting people's real needs and desires, we become immeasurably more tied to their ultimate success.

As an example, research done by the great knowledge management guru, Tom Davenport, identifies the information preferences of information executives: received from people; in context; current, correct, and concise; operational; about people (who got what); and external rather than internal. Note that this doesn't mention format or content but talks about attributes of the information process and experience. Enhance the information experience and you will be more successful. Enhance *only* the information and you won't get there.

Strategy No. 10 for Success:
Become a Transformational Librarian

Knowledge management targets both kinds of knowledge—tacit and explicit. Tacit knowledge is know-how. It is intangible, harder to adopt/learn, and generally more valuable. Explicit knowledge is about "knowing that" and "knowing what." It is tangible, able to be represented, easier to distribute, manage, and control. Many other languages separate these two concepts into two words; for example, the French words *savoir* and *connâitre.* *Connâitre* means "to know, to be acquainted with, to make the acquaintance of." *Savoir* means "to know how." A transformational librarian keeps these two aspects of knowledge in balance. Over the years, librarianship on the whole has swung too far to managing explicit information and has lost touch with our more valuable professional skills of leading or being a catalyst in the creative process of creating human beings with new tacit knowledge.

In this knowledge ecology, there is an expanded role for librarians as knowledge leaders:

1. Information pruning
2. Adding context
3. Enhancing style
4. Choosing the right medium
5. Knowledge management activities; e.g., taxonomist
6. Information audits
7. Information mapping
8. Best practice databases

9. Information literacy training
10. Skills and competencies databanks
11. Information integrity and organization
12. Licensing negotiation
13. Design and customization
14. Navigators (personal and virtual)
15. Information selection and integration skills
16. Information organization (micro and macro) skills
17. Interface selection and design, combined with training skills
18. Searching, finding, and usage skills (analysis, packaging, reporting)
19. High-level information literacy skills
20. From gatekeepers *to* gateways
21. Guide, trainer, teacher, coach
22. Team member, partner
23. Seller, marketer
24. Information ocean organizer, designer
25. Linker, qualifier, chooser, and buyer

In short, adopt "knowledge positioning." Transformational librarians focus on where the transformations occur. Transformations occur for librarians and their users primarily between information and knowledge and between knowledge and behavior. It's called learning in one case and success in the other. Transformational librarians focus on the learning organization. It's a potentially huge transformational leap to move to this perspective; the Special Libraries Association calls this "Turning Information into Knowledge and Putting Knowledge to Work." Also, by focusing on ultimate behaviors, the challenge to librarians' turf by other information and data professionals is less threatening.

CONCLUSION AND NEXT STEPS

Some final tactics are needed to start on this path to the future. My top four recommended tactics are

1. Suck up to IT [Information Technology staff members]—you need their competencies. It's probably your second most important strategic relationship.

2. Have lunch with your enterprise and market leaders and the entire breadth of potential users. Your success will be in understanding the user's real needs and goals.

3. Leave the library occasionally. It will only fall apart without you if you stay stuck there.

4. Walk and interpret—observe what your users are doing, *not* what they say they're doing. With messianic fervor, share your insights with your team.

It is absolutely true that librarians and information professionals have nearly all the competencies to thrive in the new knowledge ecology, but "insanity is doing things the way you've always done them and expecting different results" (Rita Mae Brown). [See Rita Mae Brown, *Starting from Scratch: A Different Kind of Writer's Manual* (New York: Bantam Books, 1988). Authors other than Brown have also written the same statement.] An ecology requires a healthy climate, and we can be catalysts in the ultimate health and success of the climate of the knowledge society. Remember that it was only from the perspective of the dinosaur that climatic change was a bad thing—we mammals thought it was a pretty neat change!

Abram doesn't leave out school libraries, either.

Top Five Priorities for School Libraries and Their Districts

It's all about the student—or so we keep repeating. Let's think about which technologies really improve the learner experience. We now have some pretty good track records on some new technologies that make access simpler and, therefore, we hope, better. Access, in this context, is both intellectual and physical. Intellectual access is improved when barriers to learning and adaptation of information to learning are reduced. Physical access is simply getting the information where you actually are, and it is improved when barriers that add no value to the access process are removed. Hurdles exist in both the physical and virtual worlds. Requiring a PC or specific browser to access information sets a hurdle in place in the virtual environment. Requiring information to be used within a library during specific hours is a hurdle of sorts too. Here are five key technologies that improve access in one way or another, or both.

FEDERATED SEARCH

Two of the key attributes of this Millennial generation are that they are format-agnostic—they don't choose format before seeking appropriate content—and they just don't know where to search in the first place. Libraries

From *Multimedia and Internet@Schools* 12, no. 1 (January–February 2005): 19–22. Published first by Information Today, Inc. (http://www.infotoday.com). Reprinted with permission. All rights reserved.

and vendors exacerbate the problem by using arcane language and names for the services. Does SIRS say "history" to you? Does ABI/Inform say "business"? Is Electric Library for electricians?

Less time is spent searching for information and more time using it—that's the goal of federated search technologies for learners. School districts can keep access to resources reliable and simple with subscription-based resource plug-ins providing continuous updates and a dashboard tool monitoring performance and adjusting access.

OpenURL FOR K–12!

It used to be that identifying or finding an article citation was only the beginning of a user's search for more information. But with resolvers implementing the OpenURL standard, it now marks the end of the search. OpenURL resolvers make citation information come alive by returning the full text of the article, professional reviews, author information—virtually any related information, free or licensed, to which the library has access.

In addition to time saved, students also benefit from the extra breadth and depth of information they receive via the OpenURL standard. No longer do their findings depend on their own search skills. One click on a resolver-generated OpenURL link can provide an impressive array of resources, which can include the following:

- Full-text document databases

- Abstract and index databases

- Citation databases

- Online library catalogs—both local and remote

- Content databases with reviews, tables of contents, first chapters, summaries, author biographies, etc.

- Interlibrary loan and document delivery services

- Websites—selected for value, level, and pedagogy

- Electronically accessible resources of all kinds

OpenURL resolvers are one of the supporting technologies that ensure and encourage the discovery of actual resources that support learning—not simply links and citations and pointers. It's better to implement this discovery tool at the district level rather than to tune it to the various needs of individual schools and learner groups.

FEDERATED IDENTITY MANAGEMENT

Remove the barricades! Sounds simple, but it's not. Our learners are just not seamlessly connecting to the content they need. IP authentication, passwords, library bar code numbers, and proxy servers all put hurdles between searchers and information. We need to get past this—soon! How many passwords does one person need? Two is too many in my view. Authentication hurdles add no value to the learning experience.

THE INTERFACE

Sadly, for us, there isn't one right answer to the interface issue for learning and discovery. Learners continue to come in a complex mix of intelligences and learning styles. On the positive side, this makes for a rich culture and society, but on the other hand, it creates a challenge for those of us who want to empower users in an information environment. We need the full "Swiss army knife" of interfaces to help us find and exploit information—visual interfaces, text interfaces, experiential interfaces, interpersonal interfaces, the works! In reality, however, this can't be done effectively, Renaissance-style, by letting a thousand interfaces bloom. Let's approach empowering the learner by developing a limited group of interfaces that support learners' behaviors beyond using words in search boxes. This kind of initiative needs to be developed collaboratively by cross-functional teams of professionals—experts in libraries, content, systems, curriculum design, and more. Then we need to share our successes.

THIRD-PARTY LICENSES

Rich school, poor school. Everyone should have access to a basic level of resources—electronic and print. If resources are acquired centrally, then the foundation is well set. These resources need to be integrated into the curriculum and shared across classes, schools, districts, and even states. For daily plans and units to be effective, every learner should be able to extend and improve their knowledge with the best resources available. For this to happen, three things must happen:

1. Acquire appropriate online resources throughout the district and integrate them into teaching, library, and learning strategies.
2. All resources must be accessible from home, library, and classroom.

3. The OPAC with Amazoogle-type content—book covers, links, reviews, helpful webliographies, etc.—must be supplemented. Make the OPAC an adventure, and learners will explore, discover, experience, and learn. Millions of Amazon.com and BarnesandNoble.com users, reviewers, and buyers can't be wrong!

WHY?

When schools take steps to improve access to information, the resulting benefits are huge. And having it done at the school district level (or even the state level) delivers tons of benefits over the uneven but good-hearted efforts of individual schools and libraries. Here are just a few of the benefits.

Increased use of resources. You have to believe that if learners are using more resources more often, then their learning is improving. Just like reading more improves reading and comprehension skills, using information-literacy skills more often improves that lifelong skill too. Indeed, in my experience, when federated search technologies are applied over the OPAC, selected websites, and licensed resources, the OPAC comes out on top. This is a good thing.

Better asset management. Our schools have invested millions of dollars over the years in the acquisition and management of specialized, hand-selected, curriculum-based collections. These collections are likely one of the most valuable assets owned by the school outside of the physical premises. Increasing use of them is an educational imperative.

Equity of access. Ensuring that all students, not just those attending better-funded or better-equipped schools, have access to a wealth of resources ensures that all learners have the best possible support.

Improved sharing. We learned in kindergarten that sharing is one of the cultural values that we are intended to sustain through life. With district-level effort, pricey cataloging can be copied and shared cheaply, professional cataloging can be acquired and used collaboratively, and duplicate effort is avoided.

Exchangeable collections. It's a shame that curriculum units are taught in identical time frames across the board. For example, in my kid's school, all Shakespeare is taught in the same two-month period in all grades from eight to twelve. This taxes the collections for Shakespeare essays beyond reason and rewards the students with independent resources or who get to their local school or public library first. Sadly, for the rest of the school year, these Shakespeare collections remain largely unused—what the business world would call a nonperforming asset. If collections were compartmentalized and exchanged in a cycle that allowed all students to share a larger collection, then the asset would become optimized.

More cost-effective. Buying software, maintenance, hardware, and licensed resources at the district level delivers economies of scale. Almost invariably, per-learner costs go way down.

More time- and effort-efficient. All of these technologies require a moderate degree of systems and technology talent, along with appropriate servers and maintenance. This is much more effectively done in a district's systems department environment—as long as there are commitment and understanding of the educational goals, and well-formed partnerships with talented folks who have library, subject, and teaching expertise.

We conclude with an excerpt from a recent Abram presentation.

Good Questions Generate Great Strategies

Strategic Questions for Libraries

There are more libraries in Canada than Tim Horton's and McDonald's restaurants combined: 22,000 compared to 2,049 Tim's and more than 1,200 McDonald's. And for every three donuts sold by Tim Horton's in 1999, one book or other item was accessed by someone in a library somewhere in the country. In 1999 twice as many Canadians went to libraries as to movie theaters. People go to school, public, and academic libraries more than twice as often as they go to the movies. Reference librarians in public and academic libraries answer more than seven million questions weekly.

Americans spend more than three times as much on salty snacks as they do on public libraries. They check out an average of more than six books a year. However, they spend only $25.25 a year for the public library—less than the average cost of one hardcover book.

But the future is not an extension of the past. The very things that made us successful will not ensure your future success. In fact, continuing to do the same things in the future could spell failure. Organizations must be retooled, and new skills must be learned or brought into the organization to ensure our viability. Occasionally, you must leave things behind as you evolve and move forward.

The question we should be asking is . . . What's the *best* future for libraries? There are lots of *big* questions to think about.

Presentation to the Topeka Shawnee County Public Library, February 20, 2006.

Q. What will it mean to libraries if their services can be delivered to cheap devices that almost everyone has with them all the time? Smart phones easily and cheaply offer Web, e-mail, music, talking books, e-books, etc.

A. Be creative. Design your portal to deliver just what's needed, in the format that's needed. Don't drown them!

Q. What will it mean for libraries if secure, broadband connectivity is ubiquitous in your community?

A. Be creative. Compete. Make a difference by empowering your community to take advantage. Innovate.

Q. What does it mean if a decent computer is available for under $150? Think schools, public libraries, gyms, stores, playgrounds, clubs, etc.

A. Think *transformation*. How will you empower learning, finding, and contextual experience?

Q. What does it mean if virtually all content (video, music, books, learning, courses, pictures, drawings, art) in any kind of container is available through the Internet?

Q. Do you drown, surf, or swim? How does everyone learn the skills? How do "quality and context" rise above "simple search and find"? What are the risks of satisficing?

Q. What impact will Millennials have? What about post-Millennials? These are Internet natives, not immigrants.

Q. If people and technology change, how must libraries and librarians evolve?

Q. Is your library ready and preparing for the end of the Web, the end of the browser, the extinction of DVDs, the decline of e-mail, the emergence of subscription software, the next broadband leap, the flat world, intelligent locations . . . ?

Q. What if there were no libraries? What would you do if you were starting from scratch to meet people's needs? Would your plans bear any resemblance to current plans that libraries have for the future? If libraries simply align themselves with Google, what are they missing?

Q. Who remembers that Google is focused on "search" for meeting commercial and advertisers' needs? Who's ensuring that people and entire communities have access to quality information, resources, and services; i.e., sustaining knowledge? Who's keeping in mind that discovering knowledge involves more than simply "searching and finding" content?

A. THE LIBRARY!

FIVE BIG QUESTIONS THAT REALLY MATTER

1. Have our users changed in a material way?
2. Can we relax a bit now that we've adapted to the last few *big* changes?
3. Is there another big environmental or technological change on the way?
4. Are we automating for the real future? Or are we just automating nineteenth- and twentieth-century processes?
5. Do we have the energy, resources, flexibility, and the money?

The future: in summary, by seeing the world through the lens of the customer, we create an

> opportunity to increase customer satisfaction and return visits
>
> opportunity for everyone in the organization to work to achieve the same goals efficiently
>
> opportunity to have a clear and achievable direction.

Afterword

Judith A. Siess

Okay, where do we go from here? What changes do we need to make in our libraries and ourselves? "The future is already here . . . it's just not evenly distributed yet." So said Abram in his keynote address, "Re-defining Information Quality and Value-Add in the New Information Environment," at the annual conference of the National Federation of Science Abstracting and Indexing Services on February 26, 2006. Right now, librarianship is largely made up of white middle-class women who are over forty. Some of our current users look much like us, although some are older and some are male. However, many of our users are very different from the (partially correct) librarian stereotype. They are young, racially and economically diverse, technologically savvy, and well aware of the many alternatives to using the library. The generations to come, the Millennials and post-Millennials (those in grade school now), are even more different. What's more, most of the librarians now active will retire sometime in the next twenty years—many earlier. What will the profession be like in 2025? Will we even exist as a *library* profession?

In the past I have complained that we do more introspective questioning than is either healthy or necessary. I am changing my mind. The problem is not the questioning, it's the answering. We've been answering the question by doing more of the same old, same old. Library education has been very slow to change—in admissions, philosophy, teaching style, and content. Working librarians have not embraced younger librarians and have not engaged in mentoring as actively as they should. Our workplaces have certainly not kept pace with technological and social changes. This is probably due to lack of money, but it is sometimes due to lack of will by those who fund them. Our professional organizations reinforce the dominance of the "old guard" through appointments to influential committees and other structural problems. Last, society has been slow to allow librarians to change their image from stodgy keepers of books to dynamic gatekeepers and facilitators of information. (Actually, I don't think the main product of libraries is really even information—it is answers. Answers to the questions and problems our users bring to us. Answers to problems as simple as "Where can I find a good book to read?" and as complex as "Where is the metal-finishing industry going in the next ten years?" But that's for another book.)

The Millennials bring many strengths to librarianship. However, there is a generation gap between them and the Baby Boomer librarians who dominate the professions. The situation is similar to the one in this cartoon.

© Zits Partnership. King Features Syndicate.

We must accept the Millennials as they are, then adapt to them. Their age and technological expertise and experience can bridge the gap to younger customers and help to change our image. They can reasonably expect more jobs to become available through retirements—especially in management. However, they will not have the same loyalty to their employers or the profession as their predecessors. We must adapt to them or lose them. Current librarians must listen to their ideas and help them up the ladder. Let the "new kid" go to the next conference—you've been to your share, and you can probably afford to pay your own way, too. The Millennials need to be a little patient and not expect to change the profession immediately. Many library associations have groups designed just for them, such as the New York City METRO organization's New Librarians Special Interest Group, the Conference of Newer Law Librarians of the American Association of Law Librarians, the New Members Round Table of the American Library Association, and the New Generation Policy and Advisory Group of the Australian Library and Information Association. Join them. Job security is always an "iffy" proposition, but library administrators should consider not letting the Millennials be the first to be laid off in tough times. "Who will be left to lead the library into the future?" (Rachel Singer Gordon). And we all need to make sure that our profession remains interesting, exciting, respected, and rewarding so that it can retain the best and brightest and not lose them to other information- or technology-related professions.

The future of librarianship lies in the capable hands of the next generation—and the generations after them. We, the current generation, must do whatever is necessary to pave the way for them. The future will be only as good as we *all* make it. The following is not only my favorite quotation; it is very applicable to this book.

As the Hebrew sage Hillel said, "If I am not for myself, who will be for me? If I am for myself alone, what am I? If not now, when?" We must be for our profession and ourselves—no one is going to do this for us. But we also have to be for our customers—present and future. And there is no tomorrow—the future is now!

From Abram: "To paraphrase Gandhi, 'Be the change you seek.'"

About Stephen Abram

Stephen Abram, the Vice President of Innovation at SirsiDynix in Toronto, Ontario, is a leading international librarian and lighthouse thinker in the North American library community and has extensive experience in library technology and trend forecasting, new product conceptualization, and market development. He has more than twenty-five years' experience in libraries as a practicing librarian and in the information industry. He is a frequent keynote speaker on issues that affect libraries, their communities, and librarians.

Before joining the Sirsi Corporation in 2004, where he is charged with identifying new library, end user, and information technologies and marketplace trends, Abram was with Micromedia ProQuest (formerly IHS Canada) from 1994 to 2004. He served as Director of Corporate and News Information; Senior Director of Product Management; Vice President of Strategy; and Vice President of Corporate Development. His other positions include Publisher, Electronic Information, Carswell, Thomson Professional Publishing (1992–1994); Manager and then Director of Information and Marketing Resources, and Director of Administration for the Hay Group; and Head Librarian, Coopers and Lybrand (1980–1985).

Abram was named one of the "Top 50 People Who Are Shaping the Future of Libraries and Librarianship" by *Library Journal* in 2002. He was President of the Ontario Library Association in 2002 and President of the Canadian Library Association in 2004–2005. For the Canadian Association of Special Libraries and Information Services, a division of CLA, he served as National Treasurer (1985–1988) and Toronto Chapter President (1984–1986).

He has been active in the Special Libraries Association as a member of the Toronto Chapter (President, 1990–1991), the Business and Finance Division, the Leadership and Management Division (Chair, 1992–1993), and the Information Technology Division, and was a charter member of the Information Futurists Caucus. He was on the SLA Board from 1996 to 1999, serving as Secretary for the 1997–1998 year. He has also served as Chair of the Strategic Planning and Public Relations Committees and on the influential SLA Visioning Committee. In 1995 he was named an SLA Fellow, and in June 2003 he was awarded SLA's highest honor, the John Cotton Dana Award. In addition, he received SLA's Public Relations Achievement Award in 2000 and was an SLA Toronto Chapter Member of the Year. He is President-Elect of SLA.

Abram has also been a member of the Information Technology Association of Canada (Chair, Information Industries Committee, 1994–1996), the Book and Periodical Council of Canada, the Knowledge Management Section of the Canadian Information Processing Society, the eContent Institute (Canada), and the American Library Association.

He was a founding partner of Canada Online/Canadian Information Congress (1985–1986) and has served on various conference advisory boards: Internet World, Online, Computers in Libraries, the American Society for Information Science, Internet Librarian, and Internet Librarian International. He has also been involved with the following organizations: Toronto Library Continuing Education Group (Co-chair, 1984–1999); University of Toronto, Faculty of Information Studies (1989–2006); Ryerson Polytechnic University (Lecturer, 1989–1995); and Toronto Inmagic User's Group (Founding Chair, 1985–1988). He received the University of Toronto's Faculty of Information Studies Jubilee Award in 2001.

Stephen was born in Toronto and received a B.A. (honors) in anthropology and an M.L.S. from the University of Toronto. He lives in Toronto with his author-teacher wife, Stephanie Smith Abram, and a son, Zachary, and daughter, Sydney, about whom he speaks in his lectures on the Millennials. He is an adjunct professor at the University of Toronto and a columnist for *Multimedia and Internet@Schools* and *Information Outlook.* When not working, speaking, or writing, Abram enjoys reading, making stained glass, his daughter's gymnastics, theater, and film.

Selected articles and presentations by Stephen Abram can be found at http://www.sirsi.com/Resources/abram_articles.html; and his blog, *Stephen's Lighthouse,* is located at http://stephenslighthouse.sirsi.com.

Selected Bibliography
of Abram's Work

ARTICLES AND BOOK CHAPTERS

"Are You Building Your Library with the Right Stuff?" *Computers in Libraries* 19, no. 8 (September 1999): 76–80.

"Blogging: Who Are You Reading?" *Information Outlook* 9, no. 4 (April 2005): 40–42.

"Born with the Chip." *Library Journal* 129, no. 8 (May 1, 2004): 34–37.

"Buzzwords for 2005." *Special Libraries* 84 (Fall 1993): 216.

"Celebrating Our Community: Sharing Our Values; Sharing Our Value." *Feliciter* 50, no. 3 (May–June 2004): 84–85.

"Challenge Ahead—Sustaining Our Relevance." *Information Outlook* 9, no. 1 (January 2004): 20–21.

"Channeling My Next Gen Device." *Information Outlook* 9, no. 3 (March 2005): 38.

"Charting the Future of Libraries: An Interview with Stephen Abram." *Wyoming Library Roundup,* Summer 2005.

"CLA Inaugural Address." *Feliciter* 50, no. 4 (July–August 2004): 132–34.

"Communities: From the User's Context In." *SirsiDynix OneSource,* January 2005.

"Communities: The Three R's—Roles, Relevance, and Respect." *Information Outlook* 7, no. 6 (June 2003): 37–38.

"Community Exploded." *Library Journal netConnect* (Winter 2005): 14–15.

"Competing with Google in a Special Library." *Information Outlook* 9, no. 11 (November 2005): 46–47.

"Conversation with Bill Gates." *Information Outlook* 1, no. 5 (May 1997): 23–25.

"Dealing with the Generations: New (and Free) Must-Read Studies." *Information Outlook* 7, no. 1 (January 2003): 46.

"Dressing Up and Taking Our Show on the Road." *Information Outlook* 7, no. 4 (April 2003): 23–24.

"Each One Teach One: Learning to Understand Electronic Games." *Multimedia and Internet@Schools* 11, no. 2 (March–April 2004): 18–20.

"EBooks: Rumors of Our Death Are Greatly Exaggerated." *Information Outlook* 8, no. 2 (February 2004): 14–15.

"E-Books: What Have We Learned So Far?" *SLA Toronto Chapter Courier* 41, no. 1 (Fall 2003).

"ELearning and Class Websites: Can We Actually Make Parents Happy? And Still Not Annoy Teachers, Learners and Administration?" *Multimedia and Internet@Schools* 12, no. 6 (November–December 2005): 21–22.

"E-Sustainability—The Amazing and True Story of Flavius Josephus." *Information Outlook* 7, no. 7 (July 2003): 44–45. (Written with Stephanie Smith Abram and Zachary Abram.)

"Future Conference Technologies" *Information Outlook* 7, no. 2 (February 2003): 44–45.

"Google Opportunity." *Library Journal* 130, no. 2 (February 1, 2005): 34–35.

"Google Scholar: Thin Edge of the Wedge?" *Information Outlook* 9, no. 1 (January 2005): 44–46.

"How Do We Increase Trust Using Technology?" *Information Outlook* 8, no. 5 (May 2004): 42–43.

"I'm Mad as Hell and I'm Not Going to Take It Anymore . . . A Little Fun with the Web-Challenged." *Information Outlook* 7, no. 10 (October 2003): 44–46.

"Implementing RFID: Opportunities for Libraries." *Ontario Library Association Access,* February 2004. (Written with Donna Bourne-Tyson.)

"Influence: It Takes a Fine Hand." *Feliciter* 50, no. 5 (2004): 172–73.

"Information Wants to Be Free—Bullcookies!" *Information Outlook* 8, no. 7 (July 2004): 34–35.

"Intelligent Conferences: Reality or Oxymoron?" *Searcher* 9, no. 1 (January 2001): 42–48. (Written with Rebecca Jones.)

"IP Authentication and Passwords: On Life Support and *NOT* Expected to Make It." *Information Outlook* 8, no. 8 (August 2004): 34–35.

"Is Bibliography Dead? Hell No!" *Information Outlook* 7, no. 11 (November 2003): 28–29.

"Joy of Toolbars." *Information Outlook* 7, no. 9 (September 2003): 30–31.

"Keyboards, Quill Pens, and the Future of Work." *MultiMedia and Internet@Schools* 11, no. 6 (November–December 2004): 21–22.

"KMWorld 2000: An Exponential Experience." *Information Today* 17, no. 10 (November 2000): 1, 74. (Written with Rebecca Jones.)

"Law of Unintended Consequences." *Information Outlook* 8, no. 12 (December 2003): 52–53.

"Lessons from the Past Require Your Past to Be Preserved." *Information Outlook* 8, no. 11 (November 2004): 42–43.

"Let's Talk about It: The Emerging Technology Future for Special Librarians." *Information Outlook* 6, no. 2 (February 2002): 18–29.

"Library Movement: Personal Lessons from the Front Lines." *Feliciter* 50, no. 6 (November–December 2004): 216–17.

"Library Movement: Politics, Passion and Making a Difference." *Feliciter* 51, no. 2 (April 2005): 56–57.

"Marketing Searchers in the Shifting Sands of Search." *Information Outlook* 6, no. 12 (December 2002): 44–45.

"Marketing Your Valuable Experience." *MLS: Marketing Library Services* 10, no. 7 (October–November 1996): 87–88.

"Must-See Conference Speaker." *Library Journal* 127, no. 5 (March 15, 2002): 23.

"My Top Ten Trends We Absolutely Must Track." *Feliciter* 49, no. 2 (April 2003): 66–68.

"Next Generation Interlibrary Loan: Not Even Close to Dead Yet." *Information Outlook* 9, no. 5 (May 2005): 42–43.

"Next Generation Librarians in the Workplace." In *Staff Planning in a Time of Demographic Change,* ed. Vicki Whitmell, 11–22. Medford, NJ: Scarecrow, 2005.

"Nexthead Technologies: New Ideas Worth Investigating." *Information Outlook* 9, no. 2 (February 2005): 38–39.

"No Librarians Left Behind: Preparing for Next-Generation Libraries (Part 1)." *Multimedia and Internet@Schools* 10, no. 6 (November–December 2003): 6–8.

"No Librarians Left Behind: Preparing for Next-Generation Libraries (Part 2)." *Multimedia and Internet@Schools* 11, no. 1 (January–February 2004): 17–19.

"Once More with Feeling: What Does Information Literacy Look Like in a Google World?" *Multimedia and Internet@Schools* 12, no. 3 (March–April 2005): 18–20.

"Paper and E-Paper." *MultiMedia and Internet@Schools* 12, no. 6 (November–December 2005): 21–22.

"Perfect Storm? Toto, I Don't Think We're in Kansas Anymore." *SirsiDynix OneSource,* February 2005.

"A Personal Invitation to Rediscover the Library Movement!" *Feliciter* 50, no. 4 (2004): 132+.

"Place, Space, Face, Trace." *Information Outlook* 8, no. 9 (September 2004): 38–39.

"Planning for the Next Wave of Convergence." *Computers in Libraries* 20, no. 4 (April 2000): 46–53.

"Playing to Learn! Meet and Greet the New Interactive Technologies." *MultiMedia and Internet@Schools* 12, no. 5 (September–October 2005): 16–18.

"Post Information Age Positioning for Special Librarians: Is Knowledge Management the Answer?" *Information Outlook* 1, no. 6 (June 1997): 18–24.

"PowerPoint: Devil in a Red Dress." *Information Outlook* 8, no. 3 (March 2004): 27–28.

"Primer on E-Learning . . . The Framework, the Market, the Players, Selected E-Learning Companies, Useful Links." *KMWorld* 12, no. 2 (February 2003).

"Pushing the Pay Envelope: Y2K Compensation Strategies." *Information Outlook* 3, no. 10 (October 1999): 18–24.

"Random Thoughts on Context, Content, Librarianship, and Who Is King, Exactly?" *Information Outlook* 8, no. 4 (April 2004): 42–43.

"The Really Big Picture." *OLA Access,* March 2005.

"The Role of E-Learning in the K–12 Space." *MultiMedia and Internet@ Schools* 12, no. 2 (March–April 2005): 19–21.

"Securing Our Future: Sustaining the Library Movement." *Feliciter* 51, no. 3 (2005): 96–97.

"Shift Happens: Ten Key Trends in Our Profession and Ten Strategies for Success." *Serials Librarian* (September 2000): 41–59.

"Shop Window: Compelling and Dynamic Library Portals." *SirsiDynix OneSource,* December 22, 2005.

"Simple Collaboration Tools—Quick and Easy KM." *Information Outlook* 7, no. 5 (May 2003): 44–45.

"Small Size, Big Impact: Three Stories." *MultiMedia and Internet@Schools* 12, no. 4 (July–August 2005): 22–23.

"Standards: What Do They Mean to You and Sirsi?" *SirsiDynix OneSource,* April 2005.

"Strategy Game at SLA." *Information Outlook* 2, no. 2 (February 1998): 17–21.

"Sydney Claire, SLA Professional Award Winner 2005: Transformational Librarianship in Action." *Special Libraries* 84 (Fall 1993): 213–15.

"10 R's Facing Information Professionals in Our Association." *Information Outlook* 7, no. 8 (August 2003): 28–29.

"They Can Do That?!" *Information Outlook* 6, no. 10 (October 2002): 42.

"Thinking about Phones." *MultiMedia and Internet@Schools* 13, no. 1 (January–February 2006): 21–22.

"32 Tips to Inspire Innovation for You and Your Library." *SirsiDynix OneSource,* July 5, 2005; August 3, 2005; October 26, 2005.

"Tips to Increase Innovation Capacity for You and Your Library (3 Parts)." *Information Outlook* 9, no. 8 (August 2005): 32–34; no. 9 (September 2005): 40–42; no. 10 (October 2005): 44–45.

"Top Five Priorities for School Libraries and Their Districts." *Multimedia and Internet@Schools* 12, no. 1 (January 2005): 19–22.

"Twenty Reasons for Special Librarians to Love IM." *Information Outlook* 8, no. 10 (October 2004): 40–42.

"Twenty Reasons for Teacher Librarians to Love IM." *Multimedia and Internet@Schools* 11, no. 4 (July–August 2004): 16–18.

"Twenty Ways for All Librarians to Be Successful with E-Learning." *Information Outlook* 8, no. 12 (December 2004): 42–44.

"Value of Canadian Libraries." *Letter of the Library Association of Alberta,* March 2005.

"Value of Libraries: Impact, Normative Data, and Influencing Funders." *SirsiDynix OneSource,* May 2005.

"Visualizing Language: Using Technology to Enhance Vocabulary." *Multimedia and Internet@Schools* 11, no. 3 (May–June 2004): 20–21.

"Waiting for Your Cat to Bark—Competing with Google and Its Ilk." *SirsiDynix OneSource,* September 15, 2006.

"Web 2.0—Huh?! Library 2.0, Librarian 2.0." *Information Outlook* 9, no. 12 (December 2005): 44–46.

"What about Us? The MetaLibrarian: Information for Information Pros." *Information Outlook* 8, no. 6 (June 2004): 42–44.

"What Is Your Information Outlook?" *Information Outlook* 7, no. 1 (January 1997): 34–36.

"What Will the Library of the Future Look Like? 1913–2003–2093." *Edmonton* [Alberta] *Public Library's The Source,* September 2003.

"Why Should I Care about Standards?" *Information Outlook* 7, no. 3 (March 2003): 21.

"Wireless Libraries and Wireless Communities: Why?" *SirsiDynix OneSource,* February 2005.

PRESENTATIONS

"Are You Ready for the NextHeads? Library Services for the Thumbster." Information Technology Division, Special Libraries Association Annual Conference, New York, NY.

"Born with the Chip." INFOhio, Ohio; Toronto District School Board, Toronto, ON; European Unicorn Users Group, Dublin, Ireland.

"Bridging the Gap: What Information Providers Need to Know about Information Use." University of Toronto, Toronto, ON.

"Context Is King: The Information Tornado: Toto, I Don't Think We're in Kansas Anymore." National Meeting of Information Specialists and Technical Business Analysts at CISTI, Toronto, ON; Hawaii Library Association, Oahu, HI; SirsiDynix WEBnet, Boston, MA; Alaska Library Association, Barrow, AK; Northwest ILL Conference, Portland, OR; Library Response Team, Army Library Institute, Monterey, CA; Special Libraries Association, Boston Chapter, Boston, MA; SirsiDynix Midwest Users Group, Omaha, NE; Canadian Health Libraries Association, Toronto, ON.

"Delighting the Real User: Personas in Action." Computers in Libraries, Washington, DC; Information Highways, Toronto, ON.

"Designing Products and Services." University of Toronto Faculty of Information Sciences, Toronto, ON.

"Digital Copyright: Reality Check." Association of American Publishers, Association for Library Collections and Technical Services, Canadian Library Association–American Library Association Joint Conference, Toronto, ON.

"ELearning Fundamentals and Opportunities for Info Pros." Special Libraries Association Virtual Conference.

"ELearning Overview." Computers in Libraries, Washington, DC.

"ELearning Realities for Libraries." KM World Conference, Santa Clara, CA.

"ELearning Snapshot Information." Information Highways Conference: Education Summit, Toronto, ON.

"E-Learning Tips for Internet Librarians." Internet Librarian, Monterey, CA.

"ELearning: Twenty Roles for Info Pros." Internet Librarian, Monterey, CA.

"Envision the Future: Teaching Role of Law Librarians." American Association of Law Libraries, Seattle, WA.

"E-Sustainability: Quirky Technologies, Next Generation Learners and Librarians." Alberta Library eResource Symposium, Edmonton, AB.

"Finding OZ: Discovering a Bright Future for Libraries." Metropolitan Library System Staff Event, Chicago, IL; Public Libraries Association, Boston, MA; Special Libraries Association, Cleveland Chapter, Cleveland, OH; University of Lethbridge, Alberta; Minitex Library Information Network, Minneapolis, MN; North Carolina Library Association/Southeast Library Association, Charlotte, NC; Lethbridge Public Library, Alberta; Library Association of Alberta, Jasper, AB.

"The Future beyond Google: Tech Trends for Libraries." Special Libraries Interest Group Conference, Johannesburg, South Africa; Sheridan Park Research Libraries, Mississauga, ON.

"Good Questions Generate Great Strategies: Strategic Questions for Libraries." Topeka Shawnee County Public Library, Topeka, KS.

"Growing Up Past Your Google Years: Libraries and the Next Generation of Learners." Charleston Conference, Charleston, SC.

"ILS and Library Technology Trends." American Library Association Conference, Orlando, FL.

"Informed Citizenry and Accountable Government." Library of Congress, Federal Library and Information Center Committee, Washington, DC.

"Internet at Schools." Internet Librarian, Monterey, CA.

"The Jetsons Meet the Flintstones: The Coming Collaboration Environment." Parliamentary Library, Ottawa, ON; Alliance for Innovation in Science and Technology Information, Santa Fe, NM.

"The Kids Are Alright! Millennials and Their Information Behaviors." Alaska Library Association, Barrow, AK; Association of College and Research Libraries, Minneapolis, MN; Association of College and Research Libraries, Bryn Mawr, PA; National Meeting of Information Specialists and Technical Business Analysts at CISTI, Toronto, ON; South Central SirsiDynix Users Group, Norman, OK; North Carolina Library Association, Southeast Library Association, Charlotte, NC; Special Libraries Association, Illinois Chapter, Chicago, IL.

"Law Librarians: Teaching Critical Searching Skills." Ohio Region Association of Law Libraries, Notre Dame University, South Bend, IN.

"Learning Provocations." KM World, Santa Clara, CA.

"Major Technology Trends Affecting Information Ecologies." Law Society/ Library Co., Kingston, ON.

"Measuring Success and Comparing Ourselves in an Internet Age." Charleston Conference, Charleston, SC.

"Millennials! They're Here. Deal with It!" Library Association of Alberta, Alberta; Special Libraries Association, Cleveland Chapter, Cleveland,

OH; Wyoming/Mountain Plains Library Association Conference, Jackson Hole, WY; SirsiDynix WEBnet, Boston, MA; Public Libraries Association, Boston, MA.

"Next Generation Learners." Library Association of the City University of New York Institute, New York, NY.

"Next Generation Libraries: Bricks, Clicks, and Tricks." Tennessee Library Association, Nashville, TN.

"Next Generation Searchers." Computers in Libraries, Washington, DC.

"Next Net Generation and a Technology Forecast for Special Librarians." Canadian Association of Special Libraries and Information Services, Calgary Chapter, Calgary, AB.

"The NextGen Is Different." Association of College and Research Libraries, Rutgers, NJ; Information Futurists Institute, Washington, DC.

"Open URL and Integrating Content." Internet Librarian, Monterey, CA.

"The Perfect Storm: Libraries in the Google Age." Sirsi SuperConference, Nashville, TN; Computers in Libraries, Washington, DC; Nova Scotia Public Libraries of the Future, Halifax, NS; Panhandle Library Access Network, Panama City Beach, FL; Special Libraries Association, Oregon Chapter, Portland, OR; SAILS Library Network, Cranberry Pond, MA; Knoxville Public Library, Knoxville, TN.

"Personas: The Person behind the Glass." News Division, Special Libraries Association Conference, Nashville, TN.

"Poppies, Flying Monkeys, and Good Witches: Finding the Future for Libraries." Maryland Unicorn Users Group, Maryland; Collaborative Virtual Reference Symposium, Denver, CO; New Jersey State Library, Newark, NJ; Illinois Unicorn Users Group, Joliet, IL; Connecticut Library Consortium, Hartford, CT; Southeastern Unicorn Users Group, Mobile, AL; SirsiDynix WEBnet, Boston, MA; SirsiDynix Maryland Users Group, Baltimore, MD.

"Quirky Technologies, Next Generation Learners, and Information Leaders." IntraCom 2003/Intranets 2003, Montreal, QC; Special Libraries Association, Western Canada Chapter, Vancouver, BC; Frontenac Public Library, Kingston, ON.

"Ready or Not: Emerging Technologies for Small Public Libraries." Pennsylvania North Central Libraries, Williamsport, PA.

"Real Measurements for Libraries." North Carolina SirsiDynix Users Group, Greensboro, NC; Ontario Library Consortium, Ontario; SirsiDynix Southeastern Users Group, Mobile, AL.

"Re-creating Services with New Technologies: Service Strategies for the Millennium." Medical Libraries Association, Denver, CO; Medical Library Association CE Workshop, Crystal Mountain, MI; Medical Library Association, Ottawa, ON.

"Re-Defining Information Quality and Value-Add in the New Information Environment." National Federation of Science Abstracting and Indexing Services Annual Conference, Philadelphia, PA.

"School Libraries and User Electronic Information Behaviors." Internet Librarian, Monterey, CA.

"Shift Happens: The Major Library Technology Trends and the NextGens." York District School Board, York, ON; Sirsi SuperConference, St. Louis, MS; University of Guelph Libraries, Ontario; Canadian Association of Law Libraries, Quebec, QC.

"Sustaining the Relevance of the Information Professional." Alberta Library eResource Symposium, Calgary, AB.

"Tech Trends for Libraries." Ontario Library Association, Toronto, ON; University of Cape Town, Cape Town, South Africa; Alliance for Scientific and Technical Innovation, Santa Fe, NM; Michigan Library Association, Lansing, MI; University of Memphis, Memphis, TN; Special Libraries Association, Boston Chapter, Boston, MA; Internet Librarian 2003, Monterey, CA; Special Libraries Association, ERMD Virtual Conference.

"Technology and Collaboration." Internet Librarian, Monterey, CA.

"Technology Brainstorm and Environmental Scan." Panhandle Library Access Network, Panama City Beach, FL; Information Technology Division, Special Libraries Association Annual Conference, New York, NY.

"Technoschism: Google and Our Common Future." Information Management at the Crossroads Conference, Alberta.

"TechStorm: Using Technology Intelligently to Enhance Library Service." Fraser Valley Regional Library System Staff Days, British Columbia; Southeast New York Library Resources Council, Newburgh, NY; Computers in Libraries, Washington, DC; Special Libraries Association, Illinois Chapter, Chicago, IL.

"10 Trends Rocking the Library World." Association of College and Research Libraries, Bryn Mawr, PA; Special Libraries Association, Illinois Chapter, Chicago, IL.

"Things Changed When I Wasn't Looking." Chautauqua-Cattaraugus Library System, Olean, NY; Ramapo Catskill Library System, Wallkill, NY.

"Top 10 Public Library Trends." Toronto Public Library, Expanding Our Horizons Speakers Series, Toronto, ON.

"Top Trends to Rock Your Library." Air Force/Navy Librarians Conference, Dayton, OH.

"Transformational Leadership: Leadership in the Post-Internet Age." InfoToday Conference, New York, NY; Faculty of Information Studies, University of Toronto, Toronto, ON.

"Trends and Opportunities in Reference Librarianship." Toronto Public Library Information Services Conference, Toronto, ON.

"Twenty Roles for Info Pros." Internet Librarian, Monterey, CA.

"Understanding End Users at a Deeper Level: Personas, Usability, and Norms." American Library Association, Chicago, IL.

"What Do Gartner's 2005 Predictions Mean for Libraries?" Computers in Libraries, Washington, DC.

"What's Sizzle and What's Fizzle." Sheridan Park Association, Mississauga, ON; Business and Finance Division, Special Libraries Association Annual Conference, New York, NY.

"Working with Decision-Makers: Being a Trusted Advisor in a Time of Rapid Change." Canadian Association of Special Libraries and Information Services, Toronto, ON.

"Writing for the Profession." Saskatchewan Library Association, Regina, SK.

"Year 2015: What Will Intellectual Property Look Like?" Society for Scholarly Publishing, Boston, MA.

Additional Reading

Block, Marylaine, ed. *Net Effects: How Librarians Can Manage the Unintended Consequences of the Internet.* Medford, NJ: Information Today, 2003.

Crawford, Walt. "Library 2.0 and 'Library 2.0.'" *Walt's Cites and Insights 6,* no. 2 (Midwinter 2006). http://walt.lishost.org/?p=217.

DiGilio, John, and Gayle Lynn-Nelson. "The Millennial Invasion: Are You Ready?" *Information Outlook* 8, no. 11 (November 2004): 15–22.

Federman, Mark. "Why Johnny and Janey Can't Read, and Why Mr. and Ms. Smith Can't Teach: The Challenge of Multiple Media Literacies in a Tumultuous Time." University of Toronto's McLuhan Program in Culture and Technology. [2005]. http://individual.utoronto.ca/markfederman/WhyJohnnyandJaneyCantRead.pdf.

Friedlander, Amy. "Dimensions and Use of the Scholarly Information Environment: Introduction to a Data Set Assembled by the Digital Library Federation, Council on Library and Information Resources." Outsell, November 2002. http://www.clir.org/pubs/reports/pub110/contents.html.

Gardner, Susan, and Susanna Eng. "What Students Want: Generation Y and the Changing Function of the Academic Library." *Portal: Libraries and the Academy* 5, no. 3 (2005): 405–20.

Geck, Caroline. "The Generation Z Connections: Teaching Information Literacy to the Newest Net Generation." *Teacher Librarian* 33, no. 3 (2006): 19–23.

Gordon, Rachel Singer. "The 'Bridge' Generation." *Library Journal* (November 15, 2005): 46. http://www.libraryjournal.com/article/CA6282625.html.

———. *The NextGen Librarian's Survival Guide.* Medford, NJ: Information Today, 2006.

Harris, Frances Jacobson. *I Found It on the Internet: Coming of Age Online.* Chicago: American Library Association, 2005.

Harris Interactive and Teenage Research Unlimited. "Born to Be Wired: The Role of New Media for a Digital Generation." Study commissioned by Yahoo and Carat Interactive. 2003. http://advertising.yahoo.com/summitseries/btbw_2003/.

Holliday, Wendy, and Qin Li. "Understanding the Millennials: Updating Our Knowledge about Students." *Reference Services Review* 32, no. 4 (2004): 346–66.

Howe, Neil, and William Strauss. *Generations: The History of America's Future, 1584 to 2069.* New York: William Morrow, 1991.

———. *Millennials Rising: The Next Great Generation.* New York: Vintage, 2000.

———. *13th Gen: Abort, Retry, Ignore, Fail?* New York: Vintage, 1993.

Hutley, Sue, and Terena Solomons. "Generational Change in Australian Librarianship: Viewpoints from Generation X." Presentation at "ALIA 2004: Challenging Ideas" (Australian Library and Information Association annual conference). http://conferences.alia.org.au/alia2004/pdfs/hutley.s.paper.pdf.

Johnson, Steven. *Everything Bad Is Good for You: How Today's Popular Culture Is Actually Making Us Smarter.* New York: Riverhead, 2005.

Jones, Steve, and Mary Madden. "The Internet Goes to College: How Students Are Living in the Future with Today's Technology." Pew Internet and American Life Project. September 15, 2002. http://www.pewinternet.org/report_display.asp?r=71.

Lenhart, Amanda L., Lee Rainie, and Oliver Lewis. "Teenage Life Online: The Rise of the Instant-Message Generation and the Internet's Impact on Friendships and Family Relationships." Pew Internet and American Life Project. June 21, 2001. http://207.21.232.103/PPF/r/36/report_display.asp. (See also the PowerPoint presentation at http://207.21.232.103/PPF/r/8/presentation_display.asp.)

Levin, Douglas, and Sousan Arafeh. "The Digital Disconnect: The Widening Gap between Internet-Savvy Students and Their Schools." Pew Internet and American Life Project. August 14, 2002. http://207.21.232.103/PPF/r/67/report_display.asp.

Levine, Jenny. "What Is a Shifted Librarian?" *Shifted Librarian.* May 20, 2004. http://www.theshiftedlibrarian.com/stories/2002/01/19/WhatIsAShiftedLibrarian.html.

Lippincott, Joan R. "Net Generation Students and Libraries." In *Educating the Net Generation,* ed. Diane Oblinger and James L. Oblinger. Boulder, CO: Educause, 2005. http://www.educause.edu/EducatingtheNetGeneration/5989.

McBride, Tom, and Ron Nief. *The Beloit College Mindset List for the Class of 2009.* Beloit, WI: Beloit College, 2007. http://www.beloit.edu/~pubaff/releases/mindset_2009.htm.

Murray, Neil D. "Welcome to the Future: The Millennial Generation." *Journal of Career Planning and Employment* 57, no. 3 (1997): 36–42.

Oblinger, Diana. "Boomers, Gen-Xers, Millennials: Understanding the New Students." *Educause* 38, no. 4 (July–August 2003): 37–47. http://www.educause.edu/ir/library/pdf/ERM0342.pdf.

OCLC. "White Paper on the Information Habits of College Students." 2002. http://www5.oclc.org/downloads/community/informationhabits.pdf.

Prensky, Marc. "Digital Immigrant Remedial Vocabulary." Version 1.02. June 18, 2003. http://www.marcprensky.com/writing/.

———. "Digital Natives, Digital Immigrants, Part 1." *On the Horizon* 9, no. 5 (October 2001): 1–6. http://www.marcprensky.com/writing/.

———. "Do They Really *Think* Differently? (Digital Natives, Digital Immigrants, Part 2)." *On the Horizon* 9, no. 6 (December 2001): 1–9. http://www.marcprensky.com/writing/.

Richardson, Will. *Blogs, Wikis, Podcasts, and Other Powerful Web Tools for Classrooms.* Thousand Oaks, CA: Corwin, 2006.

Smith, J. Walker, and Ann Clurman. *Rocking the Ages: The Yankelovich Report on Generational Marketing.* New York: HarperBusiness, 1997.

Steadley, Marianne. "Digital Native or Digital Immigrant: Exploring Ways to Bridge the Generational Divide in the Library." *UI Current LIS Clips.* March 2006. http://www.lis.uiuc.edu/clips/2006_03_print.html.

Stultz, Priscilla. "Generations in the Library: Eliminating the Gap." *MALL Newsletter* (Minnesota Association of Law Libraries) 32, no. 4 (January–February 2006): 4–6. http://www.aallnet.org/chapter/mall/mnews.htm.

Sweeney, Richard T. "Reinventing Library Buildings and Services for the Millennial Generation." *Library Administration and Management* 19, no. 4 (2005): 165–75.

Thomas, Chuck, and Robert H. McDonald. "Millennial Net Value(s): Disconnects between Libraries and the Information Age Mindset." Florida State University D-Scholarship Repository, Article 4. 2005. http://dscholarship.lib.fsu.edu/general/4/.

Valenza, Joyce. "The Digital Disconnect: The Widening Gap between Internet-Savvy Students and Their Schools." *Knowledge Quest* 32, no. 4 (2004): 50–55.

———. "Teens and Virtual Libraries: The Improvements They Really Want to See." *Joyce Valenza's NeverEnding Search* blog. January 4, 2006. http://joycevalenza.edublogs.org/2006/01/04/teens-and-virtual-libraries-the-improvements-they-want.

Viehland, Dennis, et al. *The 2006 New Zealand Mindset List.* Palmerston North, New Zealand: Massey University, 2006. http://mindset.massey.ac.nz.

Warlick, David. "Act Like a Native." *2 Cents Worth.* February 15, 2006. http://davidwarlick.com/2cents/2006/02/15/act-like-a-native/.

Weller, Angela. "Information Seeking Behavior in Generation Y Students: Motivation, Critical Thinking, and Learning Theory." *Journal of Academic Librarianship* 31, no. 1 (January 2005): 46–53.

Wilder, Stanley. *Demographic Change in Academic Librarianship.* Washington, DC: Association of Research Libraries, 2003. (See also *Demographic Trends in ARL Libraries.* 2004. http://www.arl.org/arl/proceedings/143/wilder.html.)

Zemke, R., C. Raines, and B. Filipczak. *Generations at Work: Managing the Clash of Veterans, Boomers, Xers and Nexters in Your Workplace.* New York: AMACOM, 2000.

Index

blogging (Con't)
  future of, 77, 79
  by Google, 94
  professional communication, 56
  and push content, 97
  search engines for, 142
  social technologies, 74
  and voyeurs, 127
Bloom, Benjamin, 50, 156
Bluetooth, 144
Blyberg, John, 80
board management. *See* human
      relations and people skills
bodily/kinesthetic learning style, 157
Bollier, David, 26–27
book lists, 129
brains and stages of technology, 70
Brand, Stewart, 26
branding, 47, 152. *See also*
      knowledge products
broadband access, free, 82
broadband connectivity, 170
Brown, Rita Mae, 163
buddy lists, 109
budgeting, 119
bulletin boards, 109
Burrus, Daniel, 39
business services, 140

C

Canadian Coalition for School Libraries,
      136
Canadian libraries, 117–118
Canadian Library Association
  Abram's inaugural address, 2005, 8–11
  Abram's presidency of, 54–56
  study of impact of school libraries, 20
candles as metaphor, 8–9
career development, 57–60, 61–65
Cartia, 150
cataloging, shared, 167
cataloging and classification, 81.
      See also folksonomies; tagging
Cavill, Pat, 9
CD-ROMs, 147–148
celebration, 52, 58
change
  and library education, 173
  pace of, 148–149

perceptions of, 46
planning for, 51–52
responses to, 68–69
in technology, 148, 170, 171
chat rooms, 145, 150, 159
cheap devices, strategies for, 170
cheapness, 51
children, 117. *See also* Millennial generation;
      post-Millennial generation
circulation statistics, 20–22
citation databases in school libraries, 165
Cleveland Public Library, 84
Click University (Special Libraries
      Association), 81
client value proposition, 152
Clifton, Joe Ann, 61–65
clinical trials, 140
Cluetrain Manifesto, 76
Clusty, 85
co-browsing, 77, 86
collaboration
  examples, 10, 79, 96
  in innovation, 97
  and leadership, 56
  tools for, 74, 100, 111
  See also partnerships
collaborative digital reference, 145, 146.
      See also virtual reference
"collaboratory," 145
collection development, 28, 95, 104
comments functionality, 77
commoditization, 160
communication devices, 81, 86
communications and e-learning, 103
communities, 108–112, 117
communities of interest, 75, 100, 110, 145,
      151–152
communities of practice, 81, 109, 111, 145
community alliances, 117, 119
community context, 32, 95, 97–98, 108–112
compensation strategies, 61–65
competencies for librarians, 3–4
competency gap, 117
competitive intelligence, 88, 140
computer literacy, 138, 140.
      See also information literacy
computer screens, 144
conference session recordings, 101
conferences, professional, 99–102
conferencing software, 111

H

Hackers' Conference (1984), 26–27
Hane, Paula J., 31–32
Haycock, Ken, 9, 19–20, 136
heart and stages of technology, 70
Holt, Glen, 16
hospital libraries, 97
human connections and Internet, 113
human relations and people skills, 36, 64, 96
human resources department, 34, 104
human/information interface, 36

I

IFLA (International Federation of
    Library Associations), 55
iKIOSK, 150
ILL (interlibrary loan), 116, 160, 165
ILS (integrated library system), 80.
    See also OPACs
ILS Customer Bill of Rights, 80
image of librarians, 61–62, 173
IMing. *See* instant messaging
information
    definition, 155
    finding vs. searching, 160–161
information, unfettered, 27–28
information age, end of, 42–43, 155
information audits, 161
information business, 39–40
information coaching, 34, 73, 137, 153, 162
information commons, 111
information design, 37
information ethics, 92
information highway, 154
information integrity, 162
information literacy
    as core competency, 3, 36, 162
    and distance education, 92, 104
    diversity in, 50
    future of, 138, 162
    and Google, 85–88
    and interoperability, 34
    in schools, 167
    and targeted search, 97
    and technology, 140, 157
    vs. training for individual applications,
    149
information mapping, 161
information organization skills, 162

information professionals, 3–5, 36.
    See also librarians and librarianship
information pruning, 161
information selection and integration, 162
information standards, 28
information technology (IT) department,
    104, 162
Ingles, Ernie, 9
innovation in technology, 97, 114, 160.
    See also technology
instant messaging
    in distance learning, 91
    and Google, 86, 94
    in library service, 81
    in Library 2.0, 79
    and PDA phones, 73
    social technologies, 74
    and Web 2.0, 77
    and workplace communities, 111
instant messaging buddy lists, 109
intangible services, 47
integrated interfaces, 158
intellectual access vs. physical access, 153
intellectual freedom, 6–7, 146
interactivity, 76–78, 111
interdisciplinary research, 112
interest groups. *See* communities of interest
interest stage of adoption, 160
interface design, 27–28, 157–158, 162, 166
interlibrary loan (ILL), 116, 160, 165
International Federation of Library
    Associations (IFLA), 55
Internet
    resources, and libraries, 152
    use of by men and women, 113
    visits to library websites, 30
    See also websites
"The Internet at School," 124–125
Internet forums as social technology, 74
"The Internet Goes to College," 17, 123
Internet skills, 140
Internet voyeurs, 127
interoperability, challenges of, 33–34
interpersonal learning style, 157
intranets
    and community, 109
    and enterprise portals, 158
    and human interactivity, 77
    in library services, 79, 140
    links to learning objects, 90

Judith A. Siess is a recognized expert in one-person librarianship and interpersonal networking. She has been the editor and publisher of *The One-Person Library: A Newsletter for Librarians and Management* since 1988 and has written six books, including *The New OPL Sourcebook: A Guide for Solo and Small Libraries* (Information Today, Inc., 2006); *The Essential OPL, 1998–2004: The Best of Seven Years of "The One-Person Library: A Newsletter for Librarians and Management,"* with Jonathan Lorig (Scarecrow, 2005); *The Visible Librarian: Asserting Your Value with Marketing and Advocacy* (ALA Editions, 2003); and *Time Management, Planning and Prioritization for Librarians* (Scarecrow, 2002). She is a member of library associations around the world and has spoken to groups of librarians in Spain, England, Germany, South Africa, Australia, New Zealand, Canada, and all over the United States. She has been an active member of the Special Libraries Association since 1980 and was the first chair of its Solo Librarians Division, which is now the fourth largest division of the association.

Jonathan Lorig is a technical systems coordinator at the Cuyahoga Community College in Cleveland, Ohio. He earned his MS in Library and Information Science from the University of Illinois at Urbana-Champaign via the LEEP online degree program. He also earned a BS in Civil Engineering at UIUC. He collaborated with Judith Siess on *The Essential OPL, 1998–2004: The Best of Seven Years of "The One-Person Library: A Newsletter for Librarians and Management"* (Scarecrow, 2005). His favorite pastimes are swimming, home improvement, and collecting reference books.